SEWING
LEATHER
accessories

How to Make Custom Belts, Gloves, *and* Clutches

SEWING LEATHER
accessories

How to Make Custom Belts, Gloves, *and* Clutches

Design Originals

an Imprint of Fox Chapel Publishing

www.d-originals.com

© 2014 by Skills Institute Press LLC and New Design Originals Corporation, *www.d-originals.com*, an imprint of Fox Chapel Publishing, 800-457-9112, 1970 Broad Street, East Petersburg, PA 17520.

Sewing Leather Accessories is an original work, first published in 2014.

Portions of text and art previously published by and reproduced under license with Direct Holdings Americas Inc.

ISBN 978-1-57421-623-3

Library of Congress Cataloging-in-Publication Data

Sewing leather accessories / the editors of Skills Institute Press.
      pages cm
   Summary: "Well-made leather accessories add flair and finesse to any wardrobe. You can experience the luxury of custom leather belts, gloves, and clutches without the custom expense. This book shows you how to sew your own finely crafted leather accessories that will last for years and years of use. With the expert techniques shared in Sewing Leather Accessories you no longer have to rely on the limited options of ready-made items. Master the basic methods and equipment used in working with leather. Learn the right way to perform every step of the process, with full-size patterns, detailed instructions, and easy-to-follow illustrated diagrams. You'll find classic, timeless projects here for making three different belt styles, fitted gloves for both men and women, and a chic clutch that also does duty as a shoulder bag. Each design can be adapted to match your personal style with endless customization options"-- Provided by publisher.
   Includes index.
   ISBN 978-1-57421-623-3 (pbk.)
   1. Dress accessories. 2. Leather goods. 3. Sewing. I. Skills Institute Press.
   TT290.S45 2014
   646'.3--dc23
                                   2013023174

To learn more about the other great books from Fox Chapel Publishing,
or to find a retailer near you, call toll-free 800-457-9112 or visit us at
www.FoxChapelPublishing.com.

Note to Authors: We are always looking for talented authors to write new books. Please send a brief letter describing your idea to Acquisition Editor, 1970 Broad Street, East Petersburg, PA 17520.

Printed in China
First printing

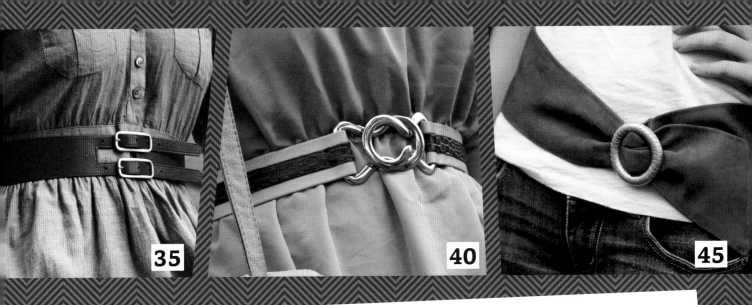

35 40 45

Contents

49 63

Introduction

Leather and other animal hides have been used for centuries, both for practical purposes, such as the construction of teepees, saddles and bridles, and for clothing and accessories, such as moccasins, bags and jackets. With such a vast history, leather can bring to mind a variety of images, from Native American garb, to cowboy chaps, to WWI bomber jackets. More recently, leather might be associated with high-fashion runways and distinct style aesthetics like punk and steampunk. No matter what associations there are with leather, there is no question that it is a great favorite as a clothing novelty and has become a pacesetter in the high-flying world of fashion.

From about 1900 to 1960, however, leather was too rare and expensive a commodity to be enjoyed by the everyday individual, and while synthetic materials were available, they were not a satisfactory replacement for the true product. Eventually, in 1964, laboratories began to produce promising substitutes for leather, made from synthetic, nonwoven fibers infused with chemical binders. These modern fakes successfully imitated the smooth texture and porous structure of leather, and turned out to be as tough and supple as real leather. In 1972, synthetic suedes also came onto the market. Soft and smooth, these pseudo suedes can be draped and molded as flatteringly as any other high-fashion fabric.

Coincidentally, with the development of such chic synthetics, the public's passion for the leather look began to grow, and it began appearing in the lines of such fashion designers as Bonnie Cashin and Anne Klein. Leather continued to appear on high-fashion runways, and also in local department stores, as advanced machinery allowed stylish new modes in leather and leather imitators to be mass-produced at a price the general public could afford.

Although leather goods can now be found worldwide in department stores, high-fashion boutiques and online, nothing can supersede the look, feel and fit of custom-made leather pieces. This book will provide you with all the information you need to know to make some of the most definitive leather fashion accessories. You will learn the characteristics of different types of animal hides and synthetics and how to prepare your material for sewing. Afterward, you will find step-by-step instructions and illustrations for making three leather classics: a pair of gloves, a belt and a clutch. Each of these items can be customized to your taste depending on the materials and colors you select to make each item, and each wearable piece will be custom made to fit you.

Try your hand at these basic projects, and you'll see there's no limit to what leather and leather imitators can do. You'll be able to fill your wardrobe with fashionable accessories in no time!

A Guide to Working with Leathers

Once you have decided to sew with real leather or fake, there are certain basic things you should know in order to select the right material for your project. The chart on pages 8–11 outlines the characteristics of various real and synthetic leathers, and indicates the basic techniques for sewing and caring for them. Additionally, on pages 12–34, you will find all the information you need for turning real leather and synthetics into garments of your choice.

While patterns usually designate fabric measured by the yard, most leather found at leather shops and fabric stores is sold by the foot. To calculate the number of square feet of leather needed, multiply the yardage suggested for your pattern by 13½ for 54-inch-wide fabric—13½ is the number of square feet in a piece of 36-inch by 54-inch fabric. Then add about 15 percent to allow for wastage. The number of square feet is marked on the back of each skin.

The same rules hold for suede, which is simply the inside layer of a cowhide, pig or lambskin, specially napped and finished.

Synthetic leathers can be a real bargain: they often cost less than half the price of natural leathers. And they are versatile: fakes successfully masquerade as leathers, suedes and reptile skins.

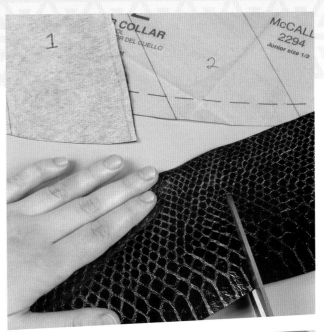

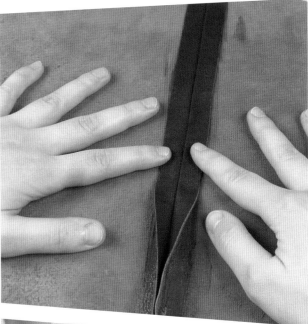

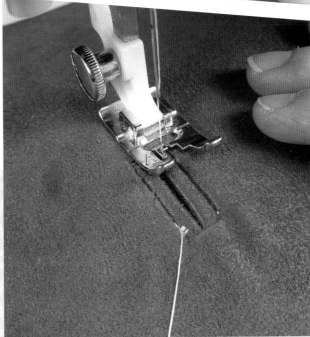

		Characteristics	Marking and Cutting
	Cowhide	Whole cowhides are available in large sizes measuring from 20 to 25 square feet. From these full hides, garments such as coats, pants and jackets can be made. However, for smaller items such as hats, handbags, belts and trim, a so-called side, or half a hide, can be purchased. The choicest part of a hide is the back, where the thickness is most uniform. Cowhide comes in medium and heavy weights and offers a wide range of colors and finishes—glossy, embossed, antiqued, sueded or disguised as another type of leather or even fabric.	Mark the back of the hide with a felt-tip pen. Hold down the pattern with weights or masking tape. Cut with regular scissors, a razor blade or a utility knife guided by a metal ruler.
	Lambskin	Lambskin is somewhat similar in texture to cowhide, though finer. The average lambskin is smaller than cow or calfhide—about 6 to 9 square feet—and more expensive. Skins are available in light and medium weights and many colors. They can be used for a variety of garments including skirts, dresses, coats and jackets—as well as for slippers, handbags and hats. Most suedes are made from the inside skin of lambs.	Mark the back of the skin, using a soft, dull pencil or tailor's chalk. Hold down the pattern with masking tape. Cut with regular scissors.
	Pigskin	Pigskin is a light- to medium-weight leather available in sueded and nonsueded finishes, and in natural and dyed colors. Most commonly it comes in natural grain, but can be embossed. Because pigskin is usually small—5 to 7 square feet—its use is generally restricted to accessories such as handbags, belts and trims.	Hold down the pattern with weights or masking tape; mark the skin with a felt-tip pen. Regular scissors are perfectly adequate to cut the average pigskin; but for thicker ones to ensure straight lines, it may be necessary to use a razor blade or utility knife guided by a metal ruler.
	Snakeskin	The skins from smaller snakes, such as the whip snake, are more delicate in texture than skins from their larger cousins—boa, cobra and python. The color of the skins varies widely; even skins of the same type may have different shades. (The glossy finish on snakeskin comes from a thin layer of varnish or plastic.) Because many skins are fragile, they are practical to use only for small items such as handbags, belts, collars and appliqué.	Reinforce the skin with iron-on interfacing such as fusible Pellon. Mark the interfaced back with a toothless tracing wheel and dressmaker's carbon paper. It is often necessary to piece several skins together to approximate the shape of your pattern. Use silk pins, making sure to insert them only in the seam allowances, as they leave holes in the skin. Cut with regular scissors.

Sewing	Pressing and Cleaning
Machine sew, using a Size 14 or 16 leather needle and heavy-duty mercerized cotton or polyester thread. Set the machine for a long stitch (7–10 stitches to the inch). Use paper clips to keep garment pieces together, removing them as you stitch. Glue down the seam allowances with rubber cement. For decoration, topstitch with a Size 16 needle and silk buttonhole twist. To create an even more sporty effect, put one raw edge over the other instead of turning the edges under, and make two rows of topstitches. Seams do not require finishing.	Press on the wrong side, using a pressing cloth and a dry iron set for low heat. If the finish is glossy or smooth, you can remove common spots and stains with a damp sponge; but leather with any other kind of finish should be sent to a dry cleaner.
Sew by machine, using a Size 11 to 14 leather needle and mercerized cotton or polyester thread. Set the machine for a long stitch (7–10 stitches to the inch). Use paper clips to keep garment pieces together, removing them as you stitch. Glue down the seam allowances with rubber cement. If you are sewing a seam that curves, cut small Vs into the seam allowance to avoid bunching the material. For decoration, topstitch the seam, using a Size 16 needle and silk buttonhole twist.	Press lightly on the wrong side, using a cool, dry iron and a pressing cloth. With colored suedes, cover the ironing board with brown wrapping paper; otherwise the heat from the iron will cause the coloring matter to soak off onto the board. To remove small spots, use a soft suede brush, gum eraser, dry sponge, terry-cloth towel or soft bristle brush. For major cleaning, send garments made from lambskin to a dry cleaner who specializes in leathers.
Sew by machine with a Size 14 leather needle and polyester or heavy-duty cotton thread. Set the machine for a long stitch (7–10 stitches to the inch). Hold garment pieces together with paper clips, removing them as you stitch. Glue down the seam allowances with rubber cement. Topstitch, using a Size 16 needle and silk buttonhole twist.	Using a pressing cloth and a dry iron set for lowest heat, press lightly on the wrong side. Like other leathers, pigskin should be dry cleaned in most cases. When the finish is smooth, however, the surface can be cleaned with a damp sponge. For dark or heavy spots, add a little mild hand soap to the water.
Sew by machine, using a Size 11 to 14 leather needle and mercerized cotton or polyester thread. Set the machine for a long stitch (7–10 stitches to the inch). Hold pieces together with silk pins inserted in the seam allowance. Glue down the seam allowances with rubber cement. The seams require no finishing.	Press on the wrong side of the skin, using a pressing cloth and a dry iron on a low setting. Too much heat removes the finish from the skin. Dry clean. For mild soiling, wipe skins clean with a damp sponge and perhaps a touch of mild hand soap.

		-------- *Characteristics* --------	---- *Marking and Cutting* -----
	Synthetic Leather	Synthetic leather is usually produced as a medium-weight fabric, commonly made with a polyurethane face and a knit or woven backing. It has a slight grain, and is readily available in a wide variety of colors, with either a dull or glossy finish. Synthetic leather can be used for any garment in place of real skins—e.g., coats, vests, pants, jackets and accessories. Caution: synthetics are vulnerable to accidental punctures and may sag out of shape.	Mark the back with a smooth-edged tracing wheel and dressmaker's carbon paper. Use silk pins to attach the pattern to the fabric, making sure to insert the pins in the seam allowances. Cut with regular scissors.
	Synthetic Snakeskin	Like synthetic leathers, snake has a fabric backing. This makes it less fragile than real snakeskins. The backing, however, also makes the fabric less pliable; thus synthetic snakeskin is best used for loose outerwear that has few darts or seams.	Mark synthetic snakeskin on the wrong side with a smooth tracing wheel and dressmaker's carbon. Use silk pins to attach the pattern to the fabric, making sure to insert the pins in the seam allowance. Regular scissors are the best tool for cutting.
	Pseudo Suedes	Synthetic suedes come in light and medium weights, and are available in a wide range of pastel and dark colors—but the fabric is relatively expensive, compared to other synthetic leathers. Lighter weights are ideal for dresses, skirts, shirts, jackets and vests. Heavyweights are good for jackets, pants and coats.	Mark the back of the fabric with a smooth-edged tracing wheel and dressmaker's carbon. Like real suede, the fabric has a nap, so be sure to buy the amount of fabric recommended for a nap layout for your pattern. Attach the pattern to the fabric with silk pins—which should be inserted in the seam allowances. Use regular scissors to cut the fabric.

Sewing	Pressing and Cleaning
Sew by machine, using a Size 14 needle and mercerized cotton or polyester thread. Set the machine for a medium-length stitch (10–12 stitches to the inch). When stitching, keep fabric pieces together with paper clips or silk pins inserted in the seam allowance. Remove the paper clips as you stitch. Glue down the seam allowances with rubber cement, then topstitch to ensure that the seams will stay flat.	Many artificial leathers cannot be pressed. Heat may break down the finish, causing a change in color or texture, and can even cause melting. Before pressing a garment, experiment with a scrap piece of fabric. Press on the wrong side, using a dry iron and a pressing cloth. Apply light pressure and low heat. Some synthetic leathers are machine washable; check the instructions for maintenance on the fabric label. If the fabric is not washable, dry clean.
As with other synthetic leathers, machine sew, using a Size 14 needle and mercerized cotton or polyester thread. Set the machine for a medium-length stitch (10–12 stitches to the inch). Stitch as you would for other synthetic leathers.	Do not press. Some types are machine washable; check the instructions on the fabric label. If the fabric is not washable, have it dry cleaned.
Machine stitch, using a Size 14 or 16 leather needle and polyester thread. Set the machine for a medium-length stitch (10–12 stitches to the inch). Hold fabric pieces together with paperclips or silk pins in the seam allowances. Remove the clips as you stitch. Secure the seam allowances with fusible web tape. Topstitch, but set the machine for a very long stitch (5–8 stitches to the inch).	As with real leather, press on the wrong side, using a pressing cloth, light pressure and a dry iron set for a low temperature. Brush to remove any pressing marks. Pseudo suede is machine washable and can also be dry-cleaned.

Adjusting Patterns for Leather

Pattern adjustment is much more important in working with leather than it is with fabrics. Care must be taken in advance to ensure a good fit, because once leather has been sewn, stitches cannot be ripped out without leaving needle marks.

Compare the pattern for your project to your own measurements, and then add or subtract inches and fractions for a perfect fit. Where you want the garment to fit tightly, allow very little ease, as the leather will stretch. On pants legs or sleeves, mark an extra inch of length to accommodate permanent creases that will develop at the elbows and knees.

After making the pattern adjustments you may want to pretest the fit of the garment before cutting into the leather. In doing so, use felt instead of muslin; felt closely approximates the bulk of leather.

LENGTHENING A PATTERN SECTION

1. Draw a pencil line at a right angle to the adjustment line marked on your pattern for lengthening or shortening. The pencil line should extend about 2 inches above and below the adjustment line.

2. Cut the pattern along the adjustment line.

3. Cut out a piece of paper slightly wider than the pattern section you are working on and about 6 inches high: draw a vertical line through its center.

4. Pin the paper to the cut-apart pattern so that the vertical lines are aligned and the pattern pieces are separated by the exact amount the section is to be lengthened.

5. Draw a new stitching line, tapering it into the original stitching line.

6. Mark and trim a new cutting edge ⅝ inch outside the new stitching line for the seam allowance.

SHORTENING A PATTERN SECTION

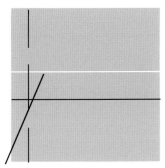

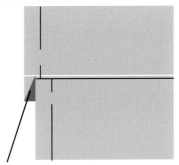

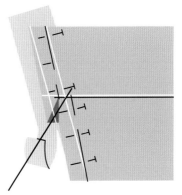

1. Draw a line above the adjustment line marked on your pattern for lengthening or shortening. The distance should be exactly equal to the amount the pattern section is to be shortened.

2. Fold the pattern so that the adjustment line meets the new line.

3. Press the fold flat with a warm iron.

4. Pin a paper extension to your pattern.

5. Draw a new stitching line, tapering it into the original stitching line.

6. Mark and trim a new cutting edge ⅝ inch outside the new stitching line for the seam allowance.

REDUCING A PATTERN SECTION

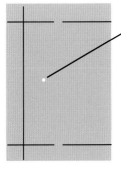

1. Divide the total amount to be reduced by the number of side seams on your garment. At the point where your pattern piece needs to be reduced, measure in from each stitching line and mark a distance equal to the resulting figure.

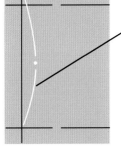

2. Draw a new stitching line, making a graduated curve from the point of reduction to the original stitching line.

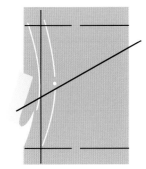

3. Mark and trim a new cutting edge ⅝ inch outside the new stitching line.

ENLARGING A PATTERN SECTION.

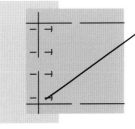

1. Lay your pattern piece on a strip of paper cut to extend about 2 inches underneath the pattern and about 2 inches beyond the edge. Pin the pattern to the paper.

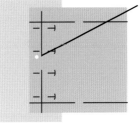

2. Divide the total amount to be enlarged by the number of side seams on your garment. At the point where your pattern piece needs to be enlarged, measure out from each stitching line and mark a distance equal to the resulting figure.

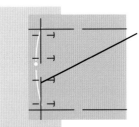

3. Draw a new tapered stitching line from the point of enlargement into the original stitching line.

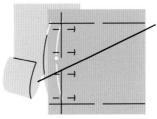

4. Mark and trim a new cutting edge ⅝ inch outside the new stitching line.

Preparation of Natural and Synthetic Skins

The craft of making leather into garments requires skills ranging from the preparation, cutting and sewing of skins to subtle ways of dealing with buttonholes and zippers.

Preparation begins with inspection of the hide for flaws and weak spots. Mark any scarred areas as shown in Box A, so that they can be avoided when laying out the pattern pieces; and reinforce weak spots with mending tape.

Suedes must be examined for the direction of the nap, and placed so that all pieces run in the same direction. Otherwise, the finished garment may appear to be composed of two different shades of suede. Snakeskin poses an additional problem; it is brittle and must be backed by interfacing.

Before you start to work on real leather, check the instructions for placement of pattern pieces (page 17). Because the direction of maximum stretch on animal hide is across the spine, those parts of the garment that receive the greatest stress should be laid out parallel to the backbone. This ensures sufficient give across the body of the garment. Because synthetic leathers have no anatomy to serve as a guide, their maximum stretch direction must be determined by the pulling method shown on page 16. Gloves, which must fit skintight, need meticulous stretching, as detailed on page 54.

PREPARING LEATHER

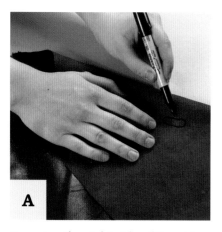

A

Examine the right side of the skin for flaws. Note the location of any unusable portions by marking the wrong side of the leather with a waterproof, felt-tip pen.

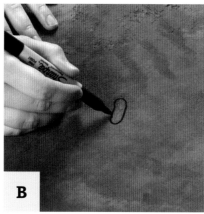

B

Turn the skin over so that its wrong side is facing up. Using the pen marks as a guide, circle the areas to be avoided when laying out your pattern.

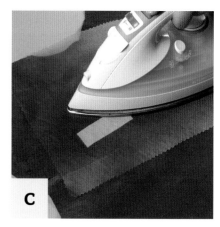

C

Reinforce any thin spots in the leather with iron-on mending tape. Affix the tape to the wrong side of the skin, using a medium-hot iron and a pressing cloth.

TRIMMING AND BACKING SNAKESKIN

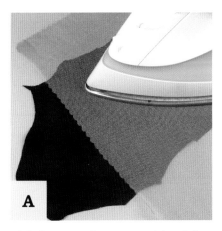

A

Lightly press the wrong side of the snakeskin with a cool iron and a pressing cloth.

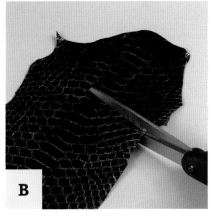

B

Trim away the unusable parts of the skin—including the head, tail and any rips or holes.

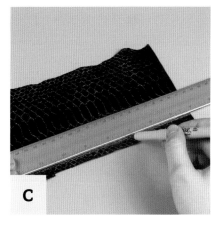

C

To make the skin a consistent width, measure it at its narrowest point. Then, draw parallel lines that distance apart from one end of the skin to the other.

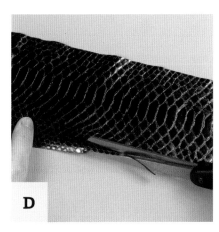

D

Trim the skin with scissors along the parallel lines.

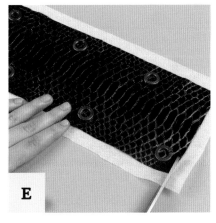

E

Using household objects to weigh it down, lay the trimmed snakeskin on a piece of iron-on interfacing. Cut the interfacing around the edges at the skin.

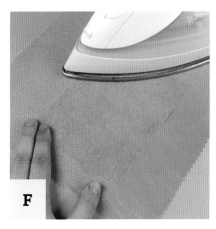

F

Fuse the interfacing to the wrong side of the snakeskin with a warm iron and a pressing cloth.

DETERMINING NAP DIRECTION ON SUEDE AND PSEUDO SUEDE

Brush your hand lengthwise over the napped surface, first in one direction, then the other. Whichever stroke feels smoothest is the direction of the nap.

Turn the skin or fabric over, wrong side up. Mark an arrow, pointing in the direction of the nap, with a waterproof, felt-tip pen.

TESTING SYNTHETICS FOR STRETCH

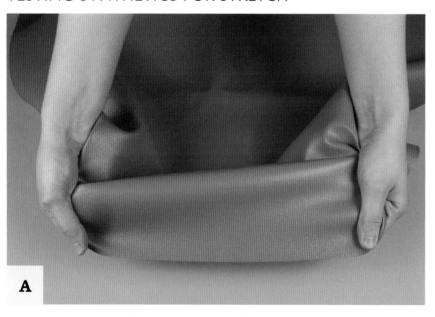

To determine which direction has more elasticity, stretch the fabric in both directions. Always cut synthetics so that the direction with the greater degree of give will be around the body.

Methods of Cutting and Marking

The most important tools for cutting leather are a utility knife and a metal ruler, although some of the lightweight leathers and all synthetics can be cut with ordinary scissors. You will also need masking tape (in place of pins) to hold down pattern pieces, and an extra-soft pencil, a felt-tip pen or a smooth-edged tracing wheel to transfer pattern markings.

With the exception of pseudo suedes, leathers and their synthetic counterparts cannot be folded without creating damaging creases. And because commercial pattern pieces are designed to be cut from a double thickness of fabric, you will have to make a duplicate of each piece before cutting. To do this, pin the pattern to brown paper bags or wrapping paper and cut out the duplicate, just as you would cut fabric; then transfer the markings of the commercial pattern to your paper duplicate with dressmaker's carbon and a tracing wheel. Be sure the carbon is under the brown paper so that your marking will produce a mirror image of the original pattern. That way you get a right and a left sleeve, instead of two right sleeves. Then, position both pattern pieces, cut them out and transfer pattern markings, observing the instructions that follow for the kind of leather you are using.

LAYING OUT AND CUTTING LEATHER

A

With the wrong side of the skin facing up, arrange the major pattern pieces along the strong, center-back portion of the skin. Smaller pattern pieces may be randomly placed wherever they fit. Be careful to avoid the marked areas indicating flaws on the skin.

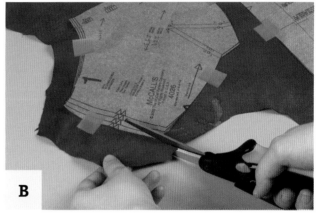

B

On lightweight leathers, secure the pattern to the skin at 6-inch intervals with masking tape. Then, cut around the edges of the pattern with scissors.

C

On heavyweight leathers, weigh down the pattern pieces with household objects. Cut around the edges of the pattern with a utility knife. Use a metal ruler as a guide when cutting straight lines.

PIECING, LAYING OUT AND CUTTING SNAKESKIN

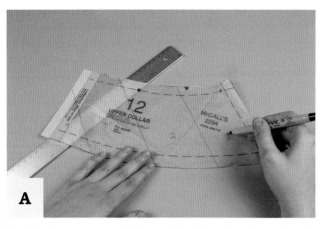

A

Decide how you want the snakeskin to be pieced and section your pattern piece accordingly. Be sure that each section on the pattern is no wider than the width of the skin less ¾ inch for seam allowances. Number each section.

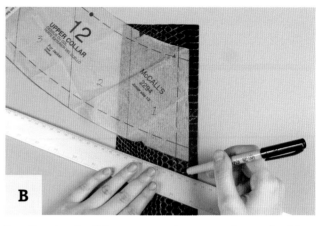

B

Lay Section 1 of the pattern piece over the snakeskin. Allowing about 1 inch extra above and below the pattern piece, draw a cutting line for Section 1.

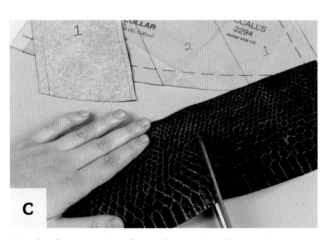

C

Cut the first section along the cutting line, and number it on the back. Cut the remaining sections in the same manner.

D

Flip the pattern piece wrong side up, and, starting again with Section 1, repeat Steps B and C for the other half of the pattern piece.

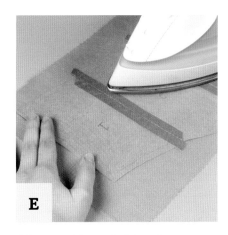

E

After machine stitching the snakeskin sections together, press open the seams with a cool iron and a pressing cloth.

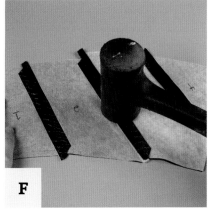

F

Apply rubber cement to each of the seam allowances. Allow it to dry, and then lightly tap the seam allowances flat with a mallet.

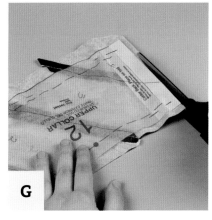

G

Pin the pattern piece within the seam allowance to the pieced snakeskin. Cut around the edges of the pattern with scissors.

LAYING OUT AND CUTTING PSEUDO SUEDE

A

Fold the pseudo suede and position your pattern pieces following the sample layouts that come with your pattern. Insert pins inside the seam allowances and use scissors to cut out the pattern pieces.

LAYING OUT AND CUTTING SYNTHETICS

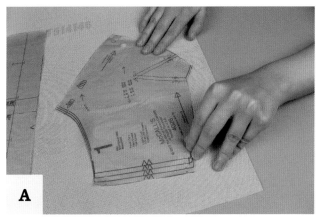

A

Pin the original and duplicate patterns to the wrong side of a single fabric thickness. Make sure their crosswise direction follows that of the greatest stretch of the synthetic (see page 16). Pin in the seam allowances. Cut with scissors.

MARKING LIGHTWEIGHT LEATHER

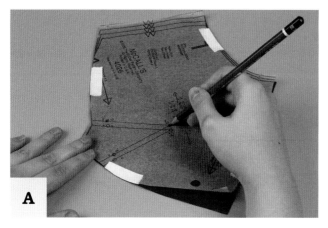

A

With a soft (No. 1) blunt pencil, pierce the pattern piece at the dot markings, transferring their location to the leather beneath.

B

Remove the pattern piece. Using a ruler as a guide, connect the pencil marks made in Step A with either a pencil or non-waxy tailor's chalk.

MARKING HEAVYWEIGHT LEATHER

A

Place a ruler on the pattern line to be marked. Fold the pattern back over the ruler to reveal the leather. With a waterproof, felt-tip pen, draw the line onto the leather along the edge of the folded pattern.

MARKING SNAKESKIN, SYNTHETICS AND PSEUDO SUEDE

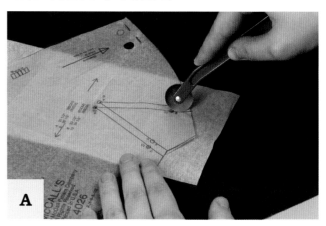

A

Using dressmaker's carbon paper and a toothless tracing wheel, trace the pattern markings onto the fabric.

Ground Rules for Stitching Leathers

Sewing seams in leather or in synthetic replicas requires dexterity, care and sometimes special tools, such as a skiver or fusing tape.

Plain seams are advisable in bulky areas where seams intersect. Top stitched seams (good for a sportier look) can be stitched with the same techniques for leather and for all fakes including the pseudo suedes. Lapped seams are suitable for real leather and pseudo suedes. Flat-felled seams are used on synthetic leathers.

In stitching and finishing leather and fakes, there are some important "do not's." Do not baste. Use pins, paper clips or glue instead, as specified on the following pages. Because pins make permanent holes, do not pin where it will show on the finished garment. Instead, pin in the seam allowances. Do not stitch on interfacing. Instead, use the heat-fusible kind of interfacing that can be pressed on with an iron. Above all, do not backstitch, because backstitching makes twice as many holes and may even create a continuous cut in the skin.

Skiving—shaving leather to make less bulky seams—requires some rehearsing. First practice on a scrap, using a special safely bevel of the kind that is available in craft stores.

MAKING A PLAIN SEAM ON LEATHER AND SYNTHETICS

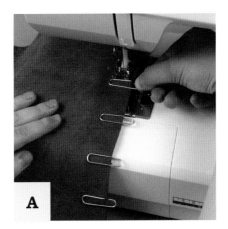

A

Place the two pieces of real or synthetic leather together, wrong sides out, with their edges aligned. Secure leather with paper clips spaced 4 inches apart; on synthetics, pin in the seam allowances. Machine stitch, using the stitching guide on the machine's throat plate to keep the seam straight.

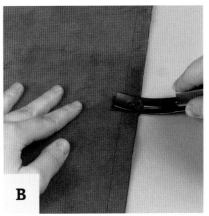

B

To reduce bulk in the seams of heavyweight leather, skive the edges of the seam allowance with a safety bevel. Hold the bevel parallel to the table, and, applying even pressure, peel away a wedge-shaped layer of the skin from the seam allowance as shown.

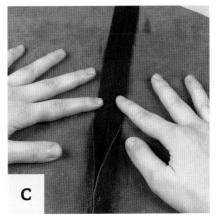

C

Brush rubber cement onto the underside of the seam allowance and onto the adjacent garment area. Let dry completely, then press the seam allowances down with your fingers.

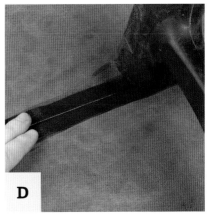

D

Flatten the seam allowances by tapping them lightly with a mallet.

MAKING A PLAIN SEAM ON PSEUDO SUEDE

A

Paper-clip and stitch the pseudo-suede seam as you would real leather. To flatten the seam allowance, cut a strip of packaged fusing tape the length of the seam and place it between the seam allowance and the garment using a medium-hot iron and a pressing cloth. Press the seam allowance flat. Brush away any marks that appear on the right side of the garment as a result of the pressing.

MAKING A TOPSTITCHED SEAM

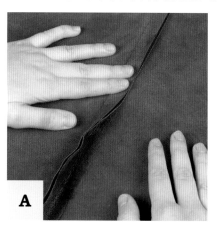

A

For light-or medium-weight leathers and synthetics, turn both seam allowances to one side and secure them with rubber cement or, in the case of pseudo suedes, fusing tape.

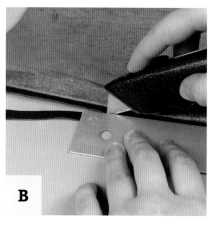

B

For heavyweight leathers, reduce bulk by first trimming one seam allowance to ¼ inch. Then fold and secure the seam as in Step A.

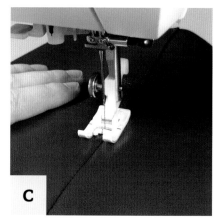

C

Turn the garment over, wrong side down, and topstitch through the outer layer and both seam allowances, ⅛ inch from the seam for light- and medium-weights and ⅜ inch for heavyweight leathers. If desired, add a second row of topstitching on lighter weights, ⅜ inch outside the first row.

MAKING A LAPPED SEAM ON LEATHER OR PSEUDO SUEDE

For leather, first trim away the seam allowance from the side that will form the overlap. Then apply rubber cement to the wrong side of the overlapping edge as shown, and to the right side of the underlapping edge.

Press the glued edges together with your fingers.

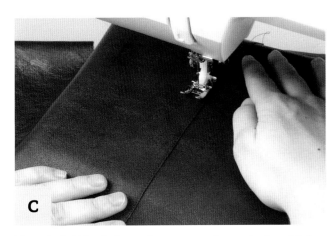

Topstitch ⅛ inch from the raw overlapped edge. Make a second row of topstitching ⅜ inch inside the first row, using the presser foot as a guide.

For pseudo suede, follow the instructions given for leather in Steps A–C, but tape the seam as illustrated here instead of gluing it. When stitching, remove each piece of masking tape just as the needle approaches it.

MAKING A FLAT-FELLED SEAM ON SYNTHETICS

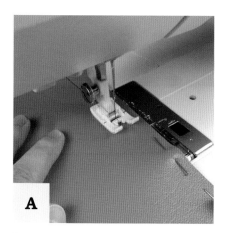

A

Lay one garment section wrong side up and place the other section wrong side down on top of it. Pin the sections together ¼ inch from the edge. Align the edge with your throat-plate guide and stitch ⅝ inch in from the edge.

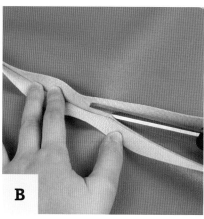

B

Spread the seam open and trim one seam allowance as close to the line of stitching as possible.

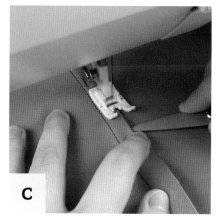

C

Fold the untrimmed seam allowance over the trimmed one and turn under ¼ inch. Then topstitch along the folded edge. Continue to fold under the edge of the fabric with the tip of a pair of scissors as you stitch.

MAKING DARTS IN LEATHER AND SYNTHETICS

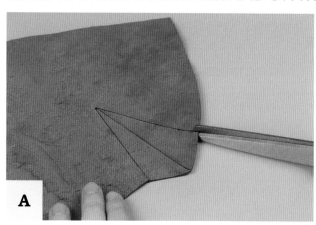

A

Make ¼-inch clips at the ends of both side lines of the dart.

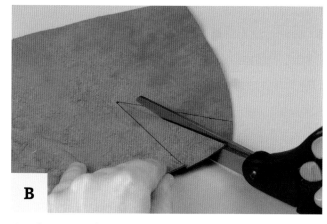

B

Cut the center line of the dart to within ⅛ inch of the point.

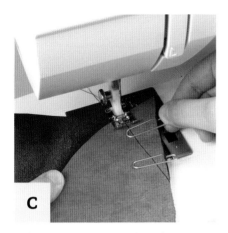

C

Fold the garment so that the ¼-inch clips are aligned. Secure the dart with paper clips (on synthetics, pin inside the seam allowance). Stitch the dart as you would on fabric, tying off the loose threads at both ends.

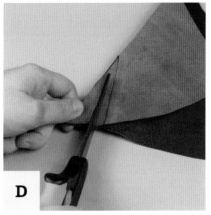

D

Trim the dart to within ⅜ inch of the stitching line.

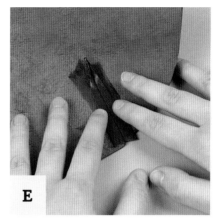

E

Apply rubber cement to the underside of the seam allowances of the dart and the adjacent area of the garment. Let the cement dry. Then press the seam allowance flat with your fingers.

MAKING DARTS IN PSEUDO SUEDE

A

Clip, pin and stitch the pseudo-suede dart as you would a synthetic leather one.

B

To flatten the point of the dart, first press the dart open with a medium-hot iron and pressing cloth. Then center a 1-inch triangular piece of iron-on mending tape over the point of the dart, as shown, aligning the apex with the dart seam. Using a tailor's ham, press the mending tape to the garment.

MAKING A POINTED COLLAR IN LEATHER

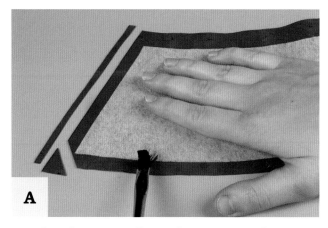

A

Interface the upper collar with iron-on interfacing. Then trim the seam allowances of the upper collar to ⅜ inch except at the neck edge. Trim the collar points diagonally to within ⅛ inch of the interfacing. Apply rubber cement to the trimmed upper collar seam allowances, and allow them to dry.

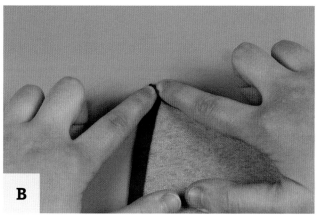

B

Turn the seam allowances back over the edges of the interfacing, pressing with your fingers. At the points, pinch the seam allowances so that the excess rises away from the collar.

C

Trim away the excess seam allowance at the points of the collar by pressing the scissor blades firmly against the collar as you clip.

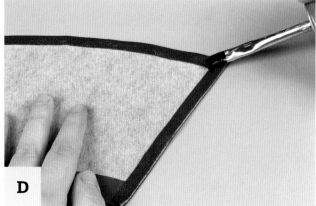

D

Apply rubber cement to the folded-over seam allowances and to the open seam allowance at the neck edge of the upper collar. Allow the cement to dry.

E

After trimming away the seam allowances of the undercollar except at the neck edge, bond it to the upper collar with rubber cement as shown.

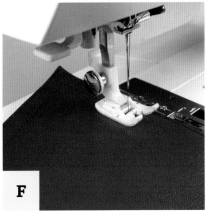

F

Make one or two rows of topstitching around the three enclosed edges of the collar ⅛ to ⅜ inch in from the edge.

G

To make a non-bulky version using heavyweight leather and pseudo suede, first cut off the seam allowances from the upper and undercollars except at the neck edge. Then interface the upper collar to within ¼ inch of its edges. Bond the upper and undercollars together with rubber cement, carefully matching their edges (on pseudo suedes, use packaged fusing tape). Topstitch the two layers together.

MAKING A HEM ON LEATHER

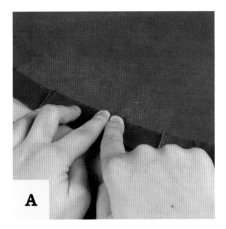

A

Brush rubber cement onto the hem allowance and the adjacent garment area. Allow the cement to dry. Turn up the hem and press it flat with your fingers. If the hem is curved, make a small pleat every few inches to compensate for the curve of the hem.

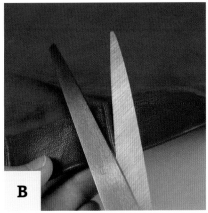

B

Trim away any pleats by pressing the scissor blades firmly against the hem as you clip.

MAKING A HEM ON PSEUDO SUEDE

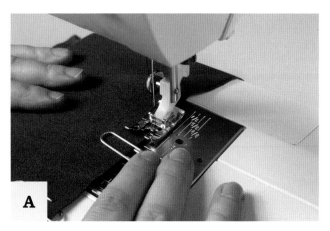

After trimming the hem so that the raw edge of the garment is the desired finished length, paper-clip a 1-inch-wide facing of the same fabric to the hem edge. Machine stitch ⅛ inch in from the edge, then again ⅜ inch inside the first row of stitching.

MAKING A HEM ON SYNTHETICS

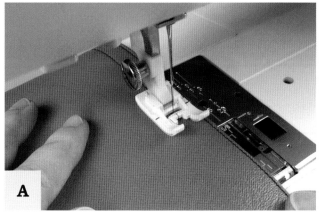

After trimming the garment edge so that the hem is ⅝ inch deep, glue the hem up with rubber cement along the hemline marking and topstitch close to the fold. Run another row of stitching ⅜ inch from the first row to catch the raw edge.

LINING LEATHER JACKETS

Because linings must be sewn in by hand and it is difficult to work on real leather by hand, first machine stitch ½-inch-wide grosgrain ribbon to the raw edges of the facing inside the garment. Sew the lining to this ribbon using a slip stitch.

Techniques for Zippers and Buttonholes

Applying zippers and buttonhole bindings to leather, synthetic skins and pseudo suedes is much easier than putting these closures onto regular fabric, because with leather, closures are always simply glued or taped on. (Conventional basting would create needle holes.) Moreover, natural leathers and the pseudo suedes need not be turned under and hemmed; their exposed raw edges give a casual, sporty appearance to the finished garment.

The centered and lapped-seam zippers in this section are hybrid versions of the kind used with regular fabric. Lapped-seam zippers are uniquely designed for leather and pseudo suedes—and are the easiest of all zippers to apply, because cumbersome seam allowances are simply cut away.

Buttonholes for the whole leather family must be done by the so-called binding technique, because the usual machine or hand stitching would leave too many close needle holes that cut the leather. Before making buttonholes on any kind of leather, be sure to reinforce the garment with interfacing. Use iron-on interfacing on leather and pseudo suede. For synthetics, glue on nonwoven Pellon interfacing.

INSERTING A CENTERED ZIPPER

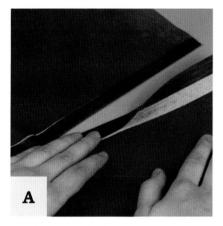

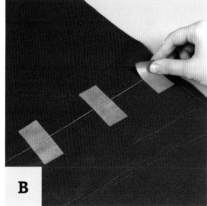

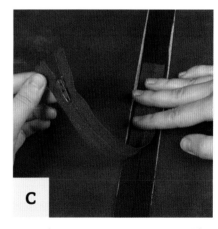

A
Machine stitch the seam up to the base of the zipper opening. For leather and pseudo suede, press iron-on interfacing under the zipper opening seam allowances; glue Pellon interfacing onto synthetics. Then, with leathers and synthetics, glue down all seam allowances, including the zipper opening; on pseudo suede, use fusing tape.

B
Turn the garment over, wrong side down, and close the zipper opening by butting the folded edges firmly together and securing them with strips of masking tape. The edge of the bottom strip of tape should align with the bottom of the zipper opening.

C
Turn the garment over, wrong side up. With leather and synthetics, apply rubber cement to the zipper opening seam allowances and the zipper tape. Allow both to dry. Then, align the zipper teeth along the zipper opening and press down with your fingers.

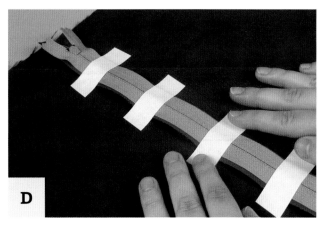

On pseudo suede, use crosswise strips of masking tape to hold the zipper in position.

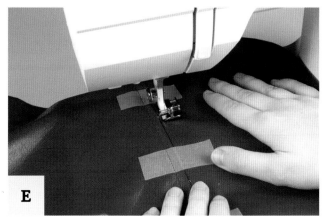

Turn the garment over, wrong side down, and, using a zipper foot, machine stitch parallel to and ¼ inch outside the zipper opening. At the base of the opening, pivot the garment and stitch for ½ inch. Pivot again and stitch along the other side of the zipper.

INSERTING A LAPPED ZIPPER

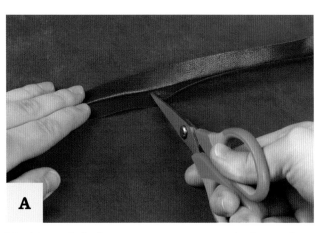

Machine stitch the garment seam up to the base of the zipper opening. Make a clip into the left-hand seam allowance ⅛ inch below the base of the zipper opening. Cut to within ⅛ inch of the seam.

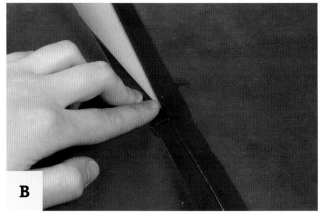

Interface the zipper opening as for the centered zipper. Then glue down the entire right-hand seam allowance and the left-hand seam allowance below the clip. Fold the free seam allowance ⅛ inch over the right-hand seam allowance.

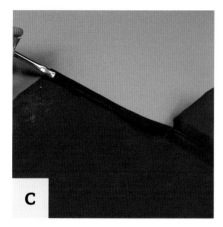

C

On leather and synthetics, push aside the right-hand seam allowance. Brush glue onto the left-hand seam allowance and the right-hand tape of the zipper. Let both surfaces dry. Pseudo suede requires no gluing at this stage.

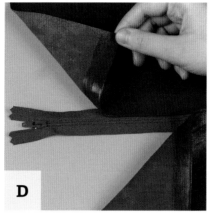

D

Place the two glued surfaces so that the fold of the left-hand zipper opening is ⅛ inch from the zipper teeth; press down. On pseudo suede, tape the zipper to the seam allowance in the same way with masking tape.

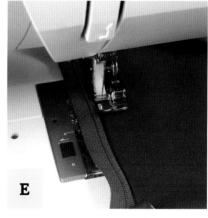

E

Using a zipper foot, machine stitch the left-hand seam allowance to the zipper ⅛ inch from the fold.

F

Close the zipper opening so that the unattached seam allowance extends ⅛ inch over the edge of the attached seam allowance. Secure it with strips of masking tape. Align the bottom strip of tape with the bottom of the zipper opening.

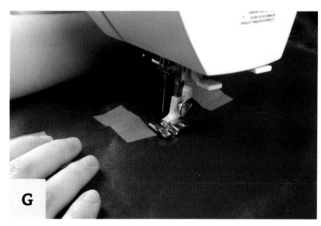

G

Using a zipper foot, topstitch ½ inch inside the fold on the overlapped edge. At the base of the zipper, pivot the garment and stitch to the seam.

INSERTING A ZIPPER IN A LEATHER OR PSEUDO-SUEDE LAPPED SEAM

A

Trim the seam allowance on the zipper underlap to ⅛ inch.

B

On leather, glue the right-hand zipper tape to the underside of the indented zipper opening ⅛ from the raw edge. On pseudo suede, tape the zipper in position. Stitch as in Step E on page 31.

C

Tape the overlapping part of the garment over the zipper so that it extends ⅛ inch beyond the edge of the zipper opening. Machine stitch ⅝ inch inside the raw edge of the overlap from the top of the zipper to the hem edge.

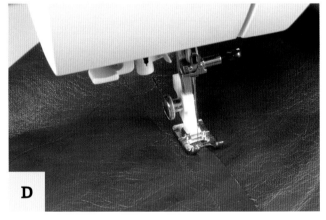

D

Stitch across the bottom of the zipper, starting at the row of stitching made in the preceding step and ending ⅛ inch from the raw edge of the overlap. Pivot the garment and continue to stitch ⅛ inch inside the raw edge of the overlap to the hem edge.

MAKING BUTTONHOLES IN LEATHER

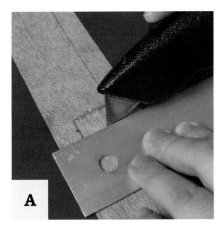

A

At the buttonhole position designated by your pattern, draw a rectangle that is the correct length for your buttons (see page 29). The width of the rectangle should be ¾ inch for heavyweight leathers and ½ inch for lightweight leathers. Mark the width of the rectangle at its center point.

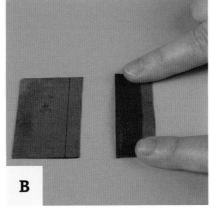

B

Cut two patches of leather that are 1 inch longer and ¾ inch wider than the buttonhole opening. Apply rubber cement to the wrong side of each patch and let it dry. Fold each patch lengthwise so that the edge of the bottom layer extends ¼ inch beyond the edge of the top layer.

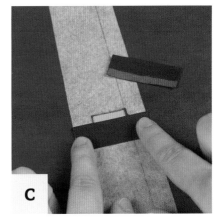

C

Apply rubber cement to the area around the buttonhole opening and let it dry. Position the folded patches, short side down, so that their folds meet at the center of the opening.

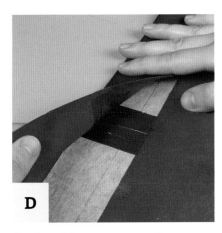

D

Apply rubber cement to the wrong side of the garment facing and to the edges of the folded leather patches. Turn the facing to the wrong side of the garment, and press it flat around the buttonhole.

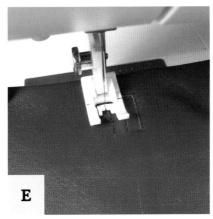

E

Turn the garment over, facing side down, and stitch around the buttonhole opening as close to the edge as possible.

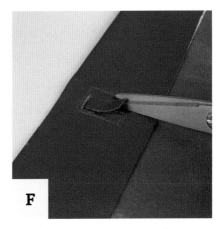

F

Turn the garment over again. Using the points of scissors to start the cut, trim away the facing ⅛ inch inside the rectangle of machine stitches.

MAKING BUTTONHOLES IN SYNTHETICS AND PSEUDO SUEDE

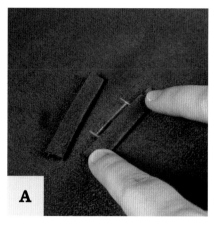

A

Cut two patches of fabric that are 1 inch longer and ½ inch wider than the pattern mark for the center placement line of the buttonhole. Fold each patch in half lengthwise, wrong sides together, and crease.

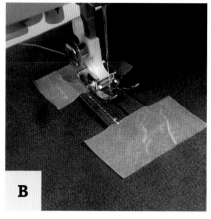

B

Position the folded patches on the garment front, so that their raw edges meet at the center placement line. Hold them with masking tape along the inside and outside placement lines, then stitch between the pieces of tape down the center of each patch.

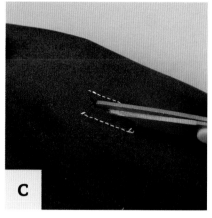

C

Turn the garment wrong side up. Using the points of scissors, make a ¼-inch-long cut at the center of the buttonhole parallel to the visible rows of machine stitching. Then make diagonal cuts from the center cut to each of the four corners of the buttonhole.

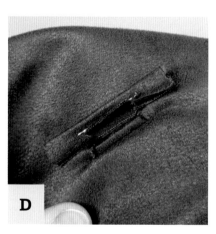

D

Turn the garment wrong side down and pull the edges of each patch through the opening to the wrong side of the garment.

E

Fold the garment along one placement line so that the patch ends extend away from the garment. Machine stitch along the placement line, catching the pointed end of the garment fabric and extending ⅛ inch above and below it. Repeat on the other placement line.

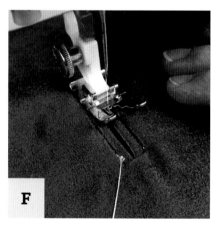

F

Turn the facing to the wrong side of the garment and insert paper clips along the outside folded edge, then stitch around the inside edges of the buttonhole to attach the facing. Cut out the facing as shown for leather (see page 33, Step F).

Double-Buckle Leather Belt

This leather belt puts a twist on an old classic by using two buckles. It is lined with medium-weight cowhide that matches the outside. Its two, tongued buckles fasten through holes made in the leather.

To make the belt holes, you will need a pair of eyelet punching pliers. For interfacing, select a medium-weight paper, such as cover stock (available in art supply stores).

This project and the ones that follow can be customized to fit your taste by changing the materials used, the colors, or the buckles. You might also adjust the width or try a synthetic leather or coated fabric.

Tools and Materials

- ❑ Leather
- ❑ Two belt buckles
- ❑ Ruler and tape measure
- ❑ Medium-weight cover stock paper
- ❑ Pencil or marker
- ❑ Scissors
- ❑ Masking tape
- ❑ Skiver
- ❑ Rubber cement
- ❑ Sewing machine
- ❑ Leather machine needle
- ❑ Leather hand-sewing needle
- ❑ Heavy-duty cotton thread
- ❑ Utility knife
- ❑ Eyelet punch

A: Determining the size of the belt

1. Place the two buckles side by side on a flat surface. Make sure that the adjacent sides are separated on their outer edges by at least ¹⁄₁₆ inch and on their inner edges by at least ⁵⁄₈ inch.

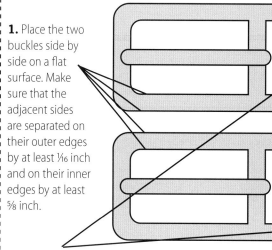

2. To determine the width of the belt, measure the distance from the upper inside edge on the top buckle to the lower inside edge on the bottom buckle.

3. To determine the length of the belt—before allowance has been made for the buckle straps at each end—begin by measuring your waist at the point where the belt will be worn.

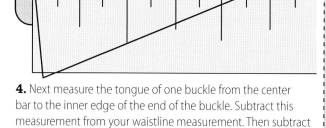

4. Next measure the tongue of one buckle from the center bar to the inner edge of the end of the buckle. Subtract this measurement from your waistline measurement. Then subtract another ¼ inch.

5. To determine the width of the buckle straps at each end of the belt, measure the inside dimensions of one buckle between the top and bottom sides.

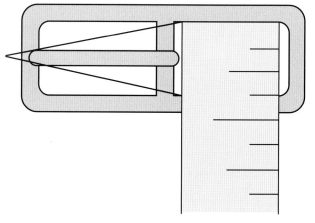

B: *Creating the pattern*

6. On a piece of medium-weight cover stock paper, which will serve both as a pattern and as interfacing, draw a rectangle to represent the belt before allowance has been made for the buckle straps. Use the dimensions determined in Steps 2–4.

paper

7. To mark the straps that will hold the buckles, begin by extending each of the long lines for 1¼ inches at one end of the rectangle.

8. Measure down from the top extension the strap width you determined in Step 5, and draw a line parallel to—and the same length as—the extension.

11. To mark the straps to which the buckles will be hooked, begin by drawing two straps as you did in Steps 7–10, but make the length of the straps three times the tongue length measured in Step 4.

12. To shape the ends of each strap into a point, start by marking the midpoint on the end of the straps.

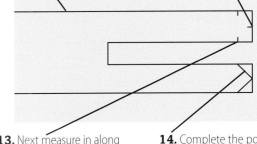

9. Connect the ends of the lines drawn in Steps 7 and 8 to complete the top strap.

10. Draw a bottom strap in the same manner.

13. Next measure in along each of the horizontal lines a distance equal to half the width of the strap, and make a mark.

14. Complete the points of the straps by connecting the midpoints with the marks made in Step 13.

15. Cut out the interfacing paper along the lines defining the shape of the belt.

C: *Cutting and marking the leather pieces*

16. Lay a piece of leather wrong side up on a flat surface.

17. To mark the belt lining, attach the interfacing paper to the leather with tabs of tape. Then, trace around the edges.

18. To mark the outside belt piece, reposition the interfacing paper, and trace around it again. Remove the interfacing paper.

19. For the outside piece only, draw cutting lines ⅜ inch outside the lines to allow for the edges to be turned up. If the space between the straps is ⅝ inch, draw one cutting line midway between them.

20. Cut out both belt pieces along the outer lines, following the directions on page 17.

21. To reduce bulk on the edges, skive an area ⅜ inch wide along all edges of both belt pieces, following the directions on page 21.

D: *Interfacing the belt*

22. Apply a thin coat of rubber cement to one side of the interfacing and to the wrong side of the leather outside belt piece. On the leather, keep the rubber cement within the inner lines as much as possible. Let the rubber cement dry until tacky.

23. Using the outline on the outside belt piece as a guide for placement, carefully adhere the interfacing to the wrong side of the outside leather piece.

24. To make sure that the pieces are bonded together securely and evenly, hit the pieces along their length with the side of your hand in a chopping motion.

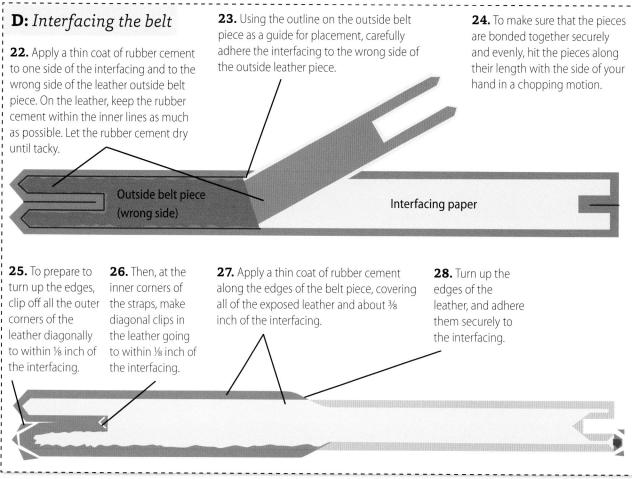

Outside belt piece
(wrong side)

Interfacing paper

25. To prepare to turn up the edges, clip off all the outer corners of the leather diagonally to within ⅛ inch of the interfacing.

26. Then, at the inner corners of the straps, make diagonal clips in the leather going to within ⅛ inch of the interfacing.

27. Apply a thin coat of rubber cement along the edges of the belt piece, covering all of the exposed leather and about ⅜ inch of the interfacing.

28. Turn up the edges of the leather, and adhere them securely to the interfacing.

E: *Assembling the belt*

29. Apply a thin coat of rubber cement to the wrong side of the belt lining and to the interfaced side of the outside belt piece. Let the rubber cement dry until tacky.

30. Adhere the lining to the outside piece, wrong sides together, working from one end to the other and making sure to align the edges carefully.

31. Secure the bond by hitting the belt along its length with a chopping motion.

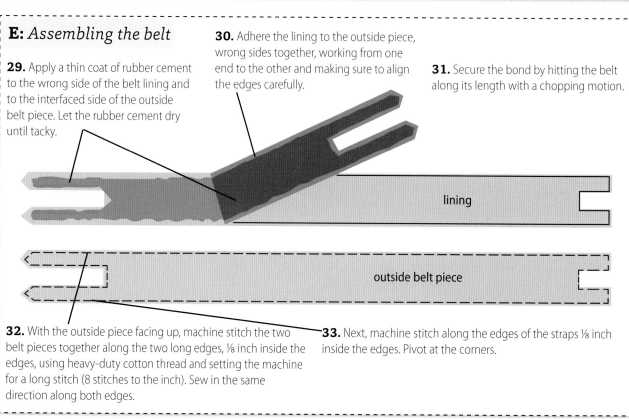

lining

outside belt piece

32. With the outside piece facing up, machine stitch the two belt pieces together along the two long edges, ⅛ inch inside the edges, using heavy-duty cotton thread and setting the machine for a long stitch (8 stitches to the inch). Sew in the same direction along both edges.

33. Next, machine stitch along the edges of the straps ⅛ inch inside the edges. Pivot at the corners.

F: *Finishing the belt*

34. To mark the opening for the tongue of the buckle, draw a rectangle on the lining side of each straightened buckle strap. The rectangle should be about ¼ inch wide and ¾ inch long, depending on the size of the hinged end of the tongue. Make sure that each rectangle is in the middle of the strap and that its inner end is aligned with the inner corner of the strap.

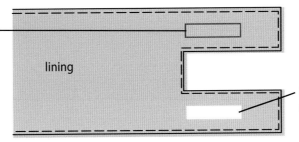

35. Using a utility knife and a steel ruler (page 17), cut the holes.

36. To attach each buckle, hold the buckle wrong side up and insert the belt strap, lining side up, through the buckle. As you do, make sure to insert the tongue of the buckle through the hole in the strap.

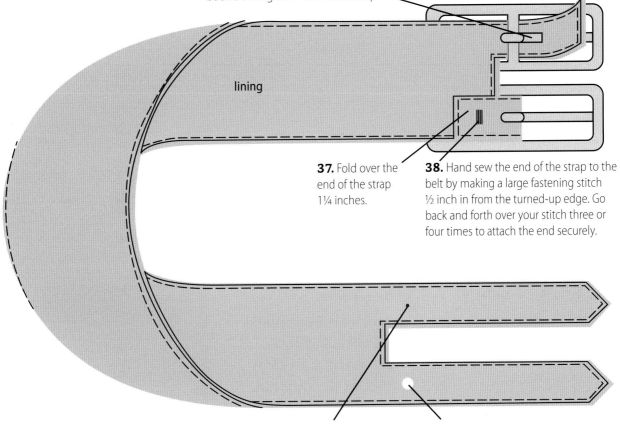

37. Fold over the end of the strap 1¼ inches.

38. Hand sew the end of the strap to the belt by making a large fastening stitch ½ inch in from the turned-up edge. Go back and forth over your stitch three or four times to attach the end securely.

39. To make the hole that each buckle will be hooked into, make a mark on the lining side of each pointed strap. Make sure that the mark is in the middle of the strap and that it is ¼ inch from the inner corner of the strap.

40. Using an eyelet punch, make a hole in each strap at the mark. The hole should be just large enough to accommodate the tongue.

Snakeskin Belt with Two-Piece Buckle

A snakeskin belt makes a great standout accent piece for an outfit, especially when paired with a unique buckle like the one shown. This belt sports a kidskin lining folded over the top and bottom of the outside. The fastener is a two-piece center clasp. Because there is no overlap, the belt must be made precisely to fit your waist.

  To make the belt holes, you will need a pair of eyelet punching pliers. For interfacing, select a medium-weight paper, such as cover stock (available in art supply stores).

A: *Determining the size of the belt*

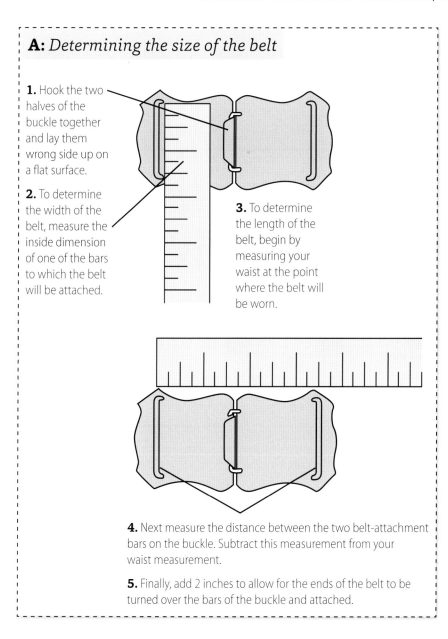

1. Hook the two halves of the buckle together and lay them wrong side up on a flat surface.

2. To determine the width of the belt, measure the inside dimension of one of the bars to which the belt will be attached.

3. To determine the length of the belt, begin by measuring your waist at the point where the belt will be worn.

4. Next measure the distance between the two belt-attachment bars on the buckle. Subtract this measurement from your waist measurement.

5. Finally, add 2 inches to allow for the ends of the belt to be turned over the bars of the buckle and attached.

Tools and Materials

- ❏ Kidskin
- ❏ Snakeskin
- ❏ Two-piece, front-clasp buckle
- ❏ Ruler and tape measure
- ❏ Scissors
- ❏ Medium-weight cover stock paper
- ❏ Pencil or marker
- ❏ Masking tape
- ❏ Skiver
- ❏ Rubber cement
- ❏ Sewing machine
- ❏ Leather machine needle
- ❏ Leather hand-sewing needle
- ❏ Heavy-duty cotton thread

B: *Cutting and marking the belt pieces*

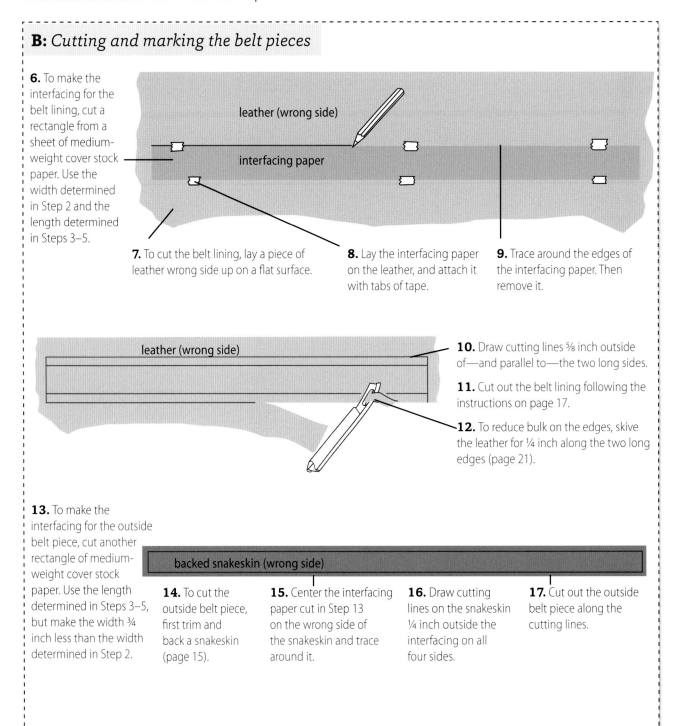

6. To make the interfacing for the belt lining, cut a rectangle from a sheet of medium-weight cover stock paper. Use the width determined in Step 2 and the length determined in Steps 3–5.

leather (wrong side)

interfacing paper

7. To cut the belt lining, lay a piece of leather wrong side up on a flat surface.

8. Lay the interfacing paper on the leather, and attach it with tabs of tape.

9. Trace around the edges of the interfacing paper. Then remove it.

leather (wrong side)

10. Draw cutting lines ⅝ inch outside of—and parallel to—the two long sides.

11. Cut out the belt lining following the instructions on page 17.

12. To reduce bulk on the edges, skive the leather for ¼ inch along the two long edges (page 21).

13. To make the interfacing for the outside belt piece, cut another rectangle of medium-weight cover stock paper. Use the length determined in Steps 3–5, but make the width ¾ inch less than the width determined in Step 2.

backed snakeskin (wrong side)

14. To cut the outside belt piece, first trim and back a snakeskin (page 15).

15. Center the interfacing paper cut in Step 13 on the wrong side of the snakeskin and trace around it.

16. Draw cutting lines on the snakeskin ¼ inch outside the interfacing on all four sides.

17. Cut out the outside belt piece along the cutting lines.

C: *Interfacing the belt*

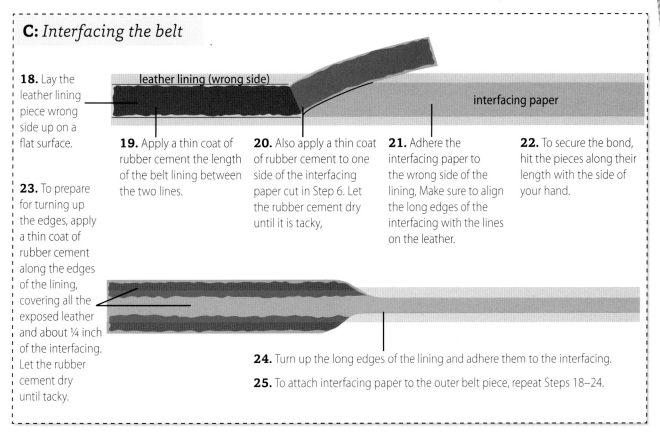

18. Lay the leather lining piece wrong side up on a flat surface.

leather lining (wrong side)

interfacing paper

19. Apply a thin coat of rubber cement the length of the belt lining between the two lines.

20. Also apply a thin coat of rubber cement to one side of the interfacing paper cut in Step 6. Let the rubber cement dry until it is tacky,

21. Adhere the interfacing paper to the wrong side of the lining, Make sure to align the long edges of the interfacing with the lines on the leather.

22. To secure the bond, hit the pieces along their length with the side of your hand.

23. To prepare for turning up the edges, apply a thin coat of rubber cement along the edges of the lining, covering all the exposed leather and about ¼ inch of the interfacing. Let the rubber cement dry until tacky.

24. Turn up the long edges of the lining and adhere them to the interfacing.

25. To attach interfacing paper to the outer belt piece, repeat Steps 18–24.

D: *Finishing the belt lining*

26. To finish the ends of the belt lining, begin by cutting from a scrap of snakeskin a strip that is ½ inch wide and ½ inch longer than the width of the interfaced belt lining.

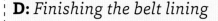
snakeskin strip (wrong side)

leather lining

interfacing

28. Glue one long side of the strip to the end of the lining on the interfaced side of the lining.

27. Apply a thin coat of rubber cement to the wrong side of the strip and for ¼ inch on both sides of one end of the belt lining. Let both dry until tacky.

29. Turn the lining over. Clip the outside comers of the strip diagonally, cutting to within ⅛ inch of the lining.

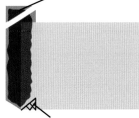

30. Turn up the two short ends of the strip and adhere them to the lining.

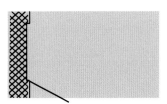

31. Turn up the long edge and glue it to the lining.

32. Finish the other end of the lining by repeating Steps 26–31.

E: *Assembling the belt*

33. Apply a thin coat of rubber cement to the interfaced side of the lining.

34. Also apply a thin coat of rubber cement to the interfaced side of the snakeskin outside belt piece. Let the rubber cement dry until tacky.

35. Using the turned-up edges of the lining as a guide, adhere the outside piece to the lining, wrong sides together. At each end, the snakeskin should extend ¼ inch beyond the lining.

36. Secure the bond by hitting the belt along its length with the side of your hand, using a chopping motion.

37. Turn the belt over so that the lining is facing up.

38. Apply a thin coat of rubber cement to the snakeskin edging at each end. Let it dry until tacky.

39. Turn up the projecting ends of the outer piece, and adhere them securely to the edging.

40. Turn the belt over so that the snakeskin piece is up.

41. Machine stitch just inside the long edges of the snakeskin piece using heavy-duty cotton thread and setting the machine for a long stitch (8 stitches to the inch). Sew in the same direction along both edges.

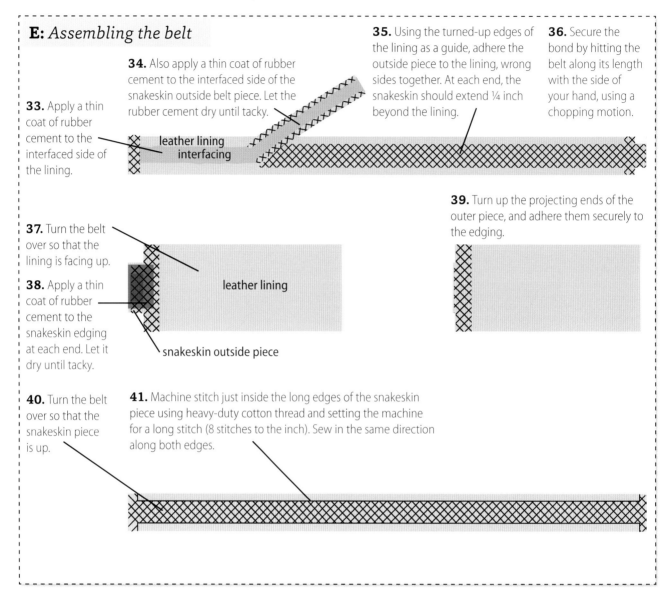

leather lining interfacing

leather lining

snakeskin outside piece

F: *Finishing the belt*

42. To attach each half of the buckle, insert one end of the belt over the belt attachment bar on the buckle half.

43. Fold the end of the belt 1 inch over the bar.

44. Attach the end of the belt by making a large fastening stitch directly over each line of machine stitching. Go back and forth over your stitch four or five times to attach the end securely.

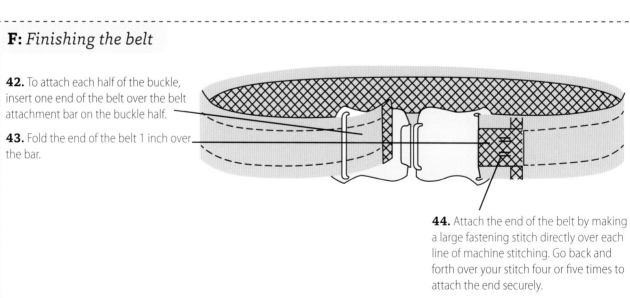

Cinched Sash Belt

This sash belt has a flirty, feminine style and can be paired with a number of garments, from a shirt to a dress. The belt is made of pseudo suede with a fabric lining. Its buckle holds the fabric in place without a tongue, so that the belt can fit any waist. Use fusible interfacing for this project.

Because this project uses pseudo suede, it can easily be customized by taking advantage of the variety of colors available. Altering the width is also an excellent way to change the look of this fashion piece.

Tools and Materials

- ❑ Pseudo suede
- ❑ Fabric for lining
- ❑ Cinch buckle
- ❑ Lightweight fusible interfacing
- ❑ Ruler and tape measure
- ❑ Pencil or marker
- ❑ Scissors
- ❑ Masking tape
- ❑ Sewing pins
- ❑ Iron
- ❑ Sewing machine
- ❑ Leather machine needle
- ❑ Leather hand-sewing needle
- ❑ Heavy-duty cotton thread

A: *Determining the size of the belt*

1. To determine the width of the belt, measure the length of the belt-attachment bar between the inner edges of the buckle. The belt should be about 2½ times wider than this measurement.

2. To determine the length of the belt, measure your waistline at the point where the belt will be worn. Then add about 10 inches.

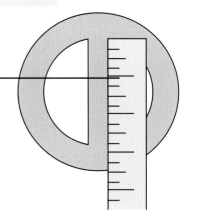

B: *Cutting and marking the belt pieces*

3. Lay a piece of lightweight iron-on interlacing, adhesive side down, on a flat surface.

4. Draw a rectangle on the interfacing, using the width you determined in Step 1 and the length you determined in Step 2.

5. At the left-hand end of the rectangle, measure in along the top side for a distance equal to half the width. Make a mark.

6. Draw a diagonal line to connect the mark made in Step 5 with the lower left-hand corner.

7. Cut out the interfacing along the diagonal line and the other three sides of the rectangle.

8. To cut out the outside belt piece, begin by laying a piece of pseudo suede wrong side up on a flat surface.

9. Lay the interfacing—adhesive side down—on the pseudo suede, and attach it with tape.

10. Using a pencil and a ruler, mark the pseudo suede by tracing around the edges of the interfacing. These lines will serve as stitching lines.

11. Remove the interfacing.

12. Draw cutting lines ⅜ inch outside of the stitching lines.

13. Cut out the outside belt piece along the cutting lines.

14. To cut the belt lining, start by laying a piece of fabric wrong side up. Lay the interfacing—adhesive side up—on the fabric so that the long edges of the interfacing are at right angles to the selvages. Pin.

15. Mark and cut the belt lining by repeating Steps 10–13.

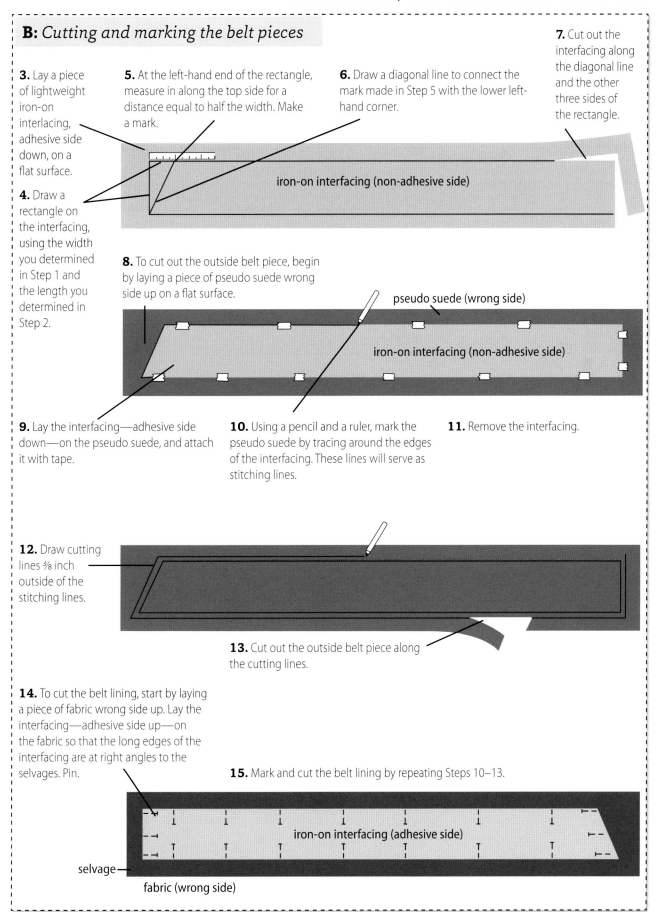

iron-on interfacing (non-adhesive side)

pseudo suede (wrong side)

iron-on interfacing (non-adhesive side)

selvage

fabric (wrong side)

iron-on interfacing (adhesive side)

C: *Assembling the belt*

16. Lay the pseudo suede outside belt piece wrong side up on a flat surface. Lay the interfacing adhesive side down on the belt piece so that the edges of the interfacing are aligned with the seam lines on the belt piece.

17. Using a hot iron. Press the interfacing onto the belt piece.

18. With the wrong sides out, pin the two belt pieces together, aligning the edges. Pin only in the seam allowances.

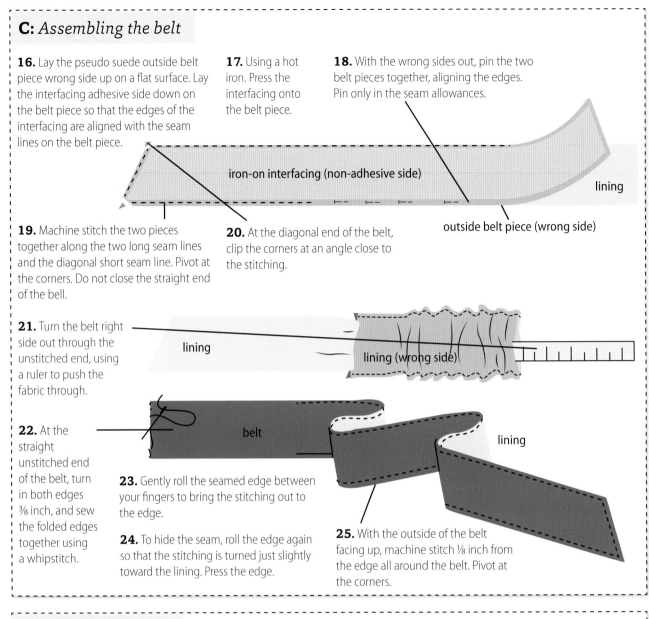

iron-on interfacing (non-adhesive side)

lining

outside belt piece (wrong side)

19. Machine stitch the two pieces together along the two long seam lines and the diagonal short seam line. Pivot at the corners. Do not close the straight end of the bell.

20. At the diagonal end of the belt, clip the corners at an angle close to the stitching.

21. Turn the belt right side out through the unstitched end, using a ruler to push the fabric through.

lining

lining (wrong side)

22. At the straight unstitched end of the belt, turn in both edges ⅜ inch, and sew the folded edges together using a whipstitch.

23. Gently roll the seamed edge between your fingers to bring the stitching out to the edge.

24. To hide the seam, roll the edge again so that the stitching is turned just slightly toward the lining. Press the edge.

belt

lining

25. With the outside of the belt facing up, machine stitch ⅛ inch from the edge all around the belt. Pivot at the corners.

D: *Finishing the belt*

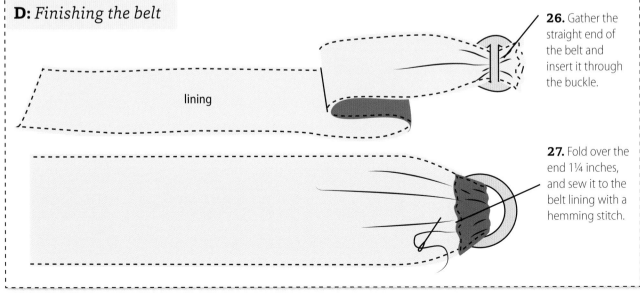

lining

26. Gather the straight end of the belt and insert it through the buckle.

27. Fold over the end 1¼ inches, and sew it to the belt lining with a hemming stitch.

Gloves

The instructions for this project provide the options for making a pair of men's gloves, a pair of women's short gloves, or a pair of women's long gloves. Each is made by cutting 10 pieces of thin leather—a stretchable synthetic may be used instead—and sewing them together with a simple running stitch. For a more formal look, slanted whipstitching can be used.

Tools and Materials

- ❏ Glove leather or stretchable synthetic
- ❏ Tracing paper
- ❏ Pencil or marker
- ❏ Ruler and tape measure
- ❏ Lightweight cardboard
- ❏ Masking tape
- ❏ Dressmaker's carbon paper
- ❏ Scissors
- ❏ Cotton cloth
- ❏ Rubber cement
- ❏ Glover's needle (leather)
- ❏ Size 7 needle (synthetics)
- ❏ Heavyweight Size B cotton thread
- ❏ Mercerized cotton thread

Preparation

These gloves can be made from any glove leather or stretchable synthetic. The most satisfactory leathers are shaved, lightweight cabretta, pigskin, kid or napa. Patterns for men's and women's gloves, including the thumb pieces, may be traced from the patterns on pages 51–53.

Before beginning, test the leather or the synthetic to determine the direction in which it stretches most readily. This will enable you to position the pattern so that the transverse direction across the knuckles follows this line. After that you will need to stretch the leather three times as you cut, to ensure that the finished glove will not stretch or sag. (Synthetics, which hold their shape, do not require this stretching.)

Begin by stretching the leather lengthwise until it will stretch no more; then cut the required glove length. Next, stretch this piece along its width—but not completely taut—until it fits the dimensions in the table on page 55. Cut the width you will need. Give the leather one more lengthwise stretch to ensure proper measurement in that direction.

The leather is now ready to be cut against the pattern and sewn with glover's needles. Synthetics can be sewn with a regular size 7 needle.

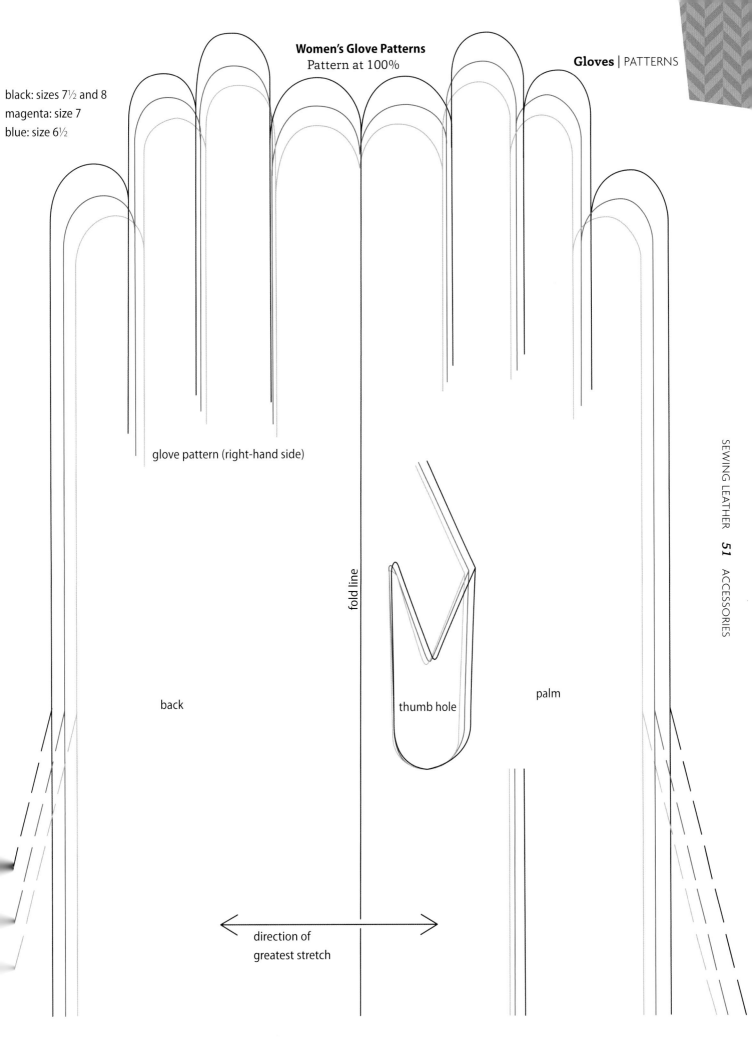

black: sizes 7½ and 8

magenta: size 7

blue: size 6½

glove pattern (right-hand side)

fold line

back

thumb hole

palm

direction of
greatest stretch

ENLARGE PATTERN 160%

Men's Glove Patterns

black: sizes 10½ and 11
magenta: sizes 9½ and 10
blue: sizes 8½ and 9
orange: sizes 7½ and 8

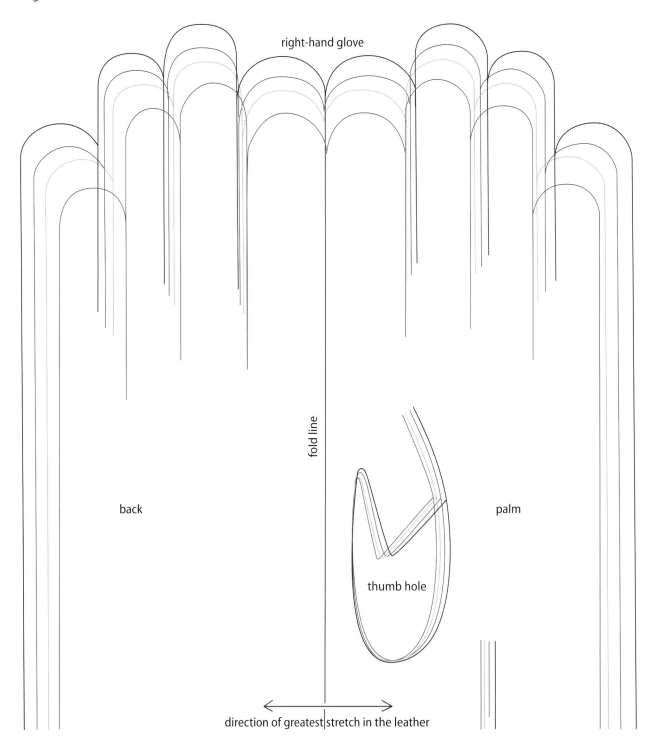

right-hand glove

fold line

back

palm

thumb hole

direction of greatest stretch in the leather

Pattern at 100%

thumb pattern (right-hand side)

direction of greatest stretch

thumb pattern (right-hand side)

direction of greatest stretch

Women's Thumb Patterns

    black: sizes 7½ and 8
    magenta: size 7
    blue: size 6½

Men's Thumb Patterns

    black: sizes 10½ and 11
    magenta: sizes 9½ and 10
    blue: sizes 8½ and 9
    orange: sizes 7½ and 8

CUTTING THE PATTERN

1. Pick the outline for the glove size you wish to make from among the patterns on pages 51–52.

2. Using tracing paper, copy the outline you select together with the center fold line and the vent line. For a woman's wrist-length glove, trace the solid straight lines on the sides. For a longer woman's glove—which will have a flared opening—trace the outward-sloping dash lines, and ignore the vent line.

3. At the bottom, extend the side lines and the center fold and vent lines about 2 inches for wrist-length gloves, and up to 8 inches for longer ones.

4. To mark the hem cutting line, measure down from the bottom of the thumbhole 2½ inches for wrist-length gloves. For long flared gloves, measure down for whatever length suits you. Then draw a line at a right angle to the fold line.

tracing paper

fold line

grain-line arrow

hem cutting line

5. Place the tracing paper, marked side up, on a piece of lightweight cardboard. Use tabs of tape to hold it in place.

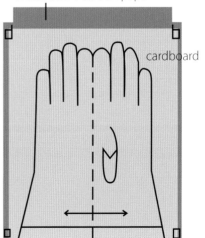

dressmaker's carbon paper

cardboard

6. Insert dressmaker's carbon paper between the tracing paper and the cardboard, and transfer the glove outline and all markings to the cardboard.

CUTTING THE PATTERN

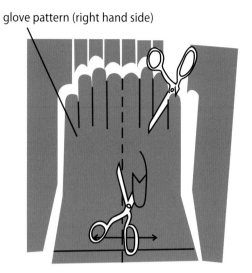

glove pattern (right hand side)

7. Remove the tracing paper, and write "right-hand glove" on the marked side of the cardboard. Write "left-hand glove" on the other side.

8. Cut the pattern from the cardboard along the lines.

9. To cut out the thumb pattern, repeat Steps 1–8 using the outlines on page 53.

CUTTING THE LEATHER PIECES

A: *Dampening the leather*

1. To determine the direction of greatest give, test the leather by stretching it. On most skins, there will be more give in the side-to-side direction than the head-to-tail direction.

2. Using a pencil, mark the direction of maximum stretch with several grain-line arrows on the wrong side of the leather.

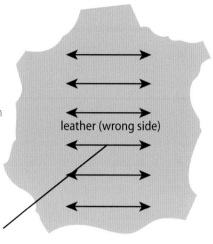

leather (wrong side)

3. To dampen the leather so that it will hold its stretch, begin by wetting a thin cotton cloth. Wring it out thoroughly so that it is only slightly damp, making sure to remove all the excess water. Then spread the cloth on a flat surface.

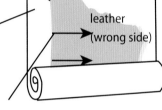

fold   damp cloth

leather (wrong side)

4. Fold the leather in half so that the wrong side is out, and lay it on the damp cloth.

5. Tightly roll up the leather in the cloth. Leave thin leather rolled up for about 10 minutes. For heavier leather, leave it for 15 minutes.

6. Unroll the leather, and remove the cloth.

B: *Stretching the leather*

7. To stretch the leather, place it wrong side down over the edge of a table so that the grain-line arrows are parallel to the table edge. Then, while holding it flat against the tabletop with one hand, grasp the lower end of the leather with the other hand, and pull it several times forcefully. Continue stretching the leather in this manner until it has no give left. Shift the position of the leather on the table edge occasionally, and rotate it 180° at least once. Make sure it is stretched evenly along the edges as well as in the center.

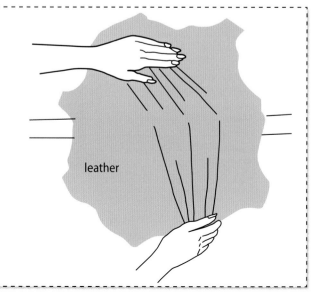

leather

C: *Cutting the leather*

8. Lay the stretched skin, wrong side up, on a flat surface and smooth out the wrinkles.

9. To determine the width of the leather strip needed for the gloves, measure your pattern from the lip of the middle finger to the hem edge. Then add 1 inch.

10. Cut a leather strip to the width you determined in Step 9. Make sure your cut is parallel to the grain-line arrows.

11. Turn the leather strip over so that the wrong side faces down. Then stretch the strip by repeating Step 7, this time stretching the leather in the direction of the grain-line arrows. Stop when the width of the strip narrows to the measurement shown below. If the strip will not stretch enough, dampen it again by repeating Steps 3–6.

Width before stretching	Width after stretching
10 inches	6 inches
11 inches	6¾ inches
12 inches	7¼ inches
13 inches	8 inches

12. Lay the stretched leather strip wrong side up on a flat surface, and smooth out the wrinkles.

13. To determine the size of the piece you will need to cut from the leather strip for each glove, add 1 inch to the size number of the gloves. (For example, if you are making size 7 gloves, the measurement would be 8 inches.)

14. If you are making wrist-length gloves, cut two pieces from the leather strip to the dimension determined in Step 13. Make sure the new cuts are at right angles to the cut edges of the strip. Then skip to Box D.

15. If you are making long flared gloves, draw two parallel lines on the strip separated by the distance you determined in Step 13. Make sure the lines are at right angles to the cut edges.

16. Determine how much flare you should add. Use 1½ inches if the hem cutting line on your pattern is 3 inches below the bottom of the thumb hole. Add ⅛ inch for each additional inch of glove length.

17. Along one cut edge of the strip, measure out from each line the distance you determined in Step 16 and make a mark.

18. Starting at the other cut edge, measure down 3 inches along each line and make a mark.

19. Draw lines to connect the marks made in Steps 17 and 18.

20. Cut out the leather piece along the lines as shown.

21. Repeal Steps 15–20 to cut out the other glove piece.

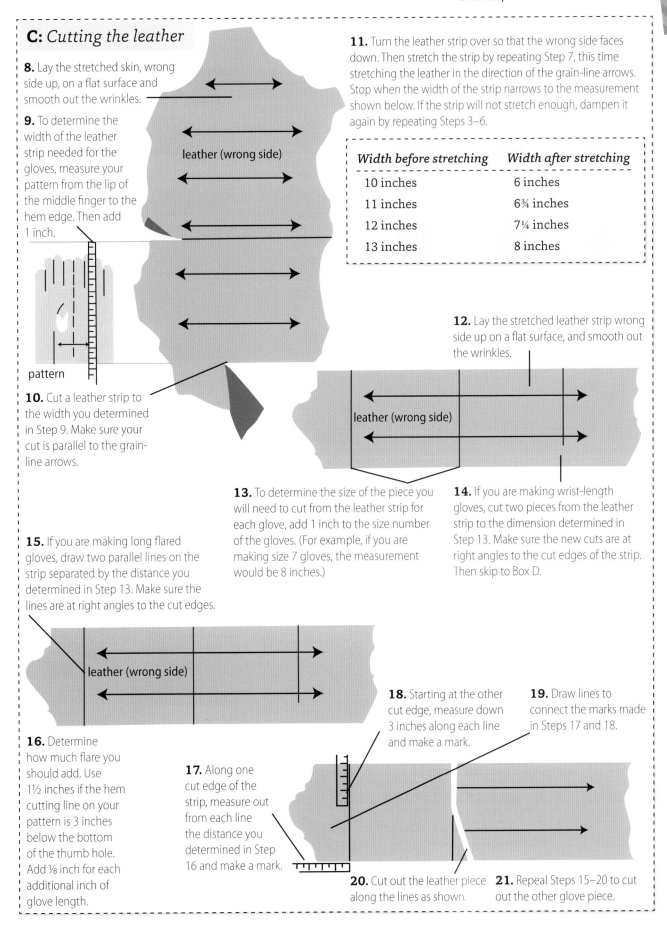

pattern

leather (wrong side)

D: *Cutting the gloves pieces*

22. Stretch one leather piece in the direction opposite the grain-line arrows. Stop when the piece is slightly narrower than the pattern.

23. Place the pattern on a flat surface so that the side marked "left-hand glove" is facing up. Lay the stretched leather piece, wrong side down, over it so that the grain-line arrows on the pattern and the leather piece are parallel.

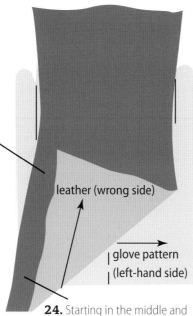

leather (wrong side)

glove pattern (left-hand side)

24. Starting in the middle and working out to the sides, smooth and stretch the leather until the edges of the leather align exactly with the side edges of the pattern.

25. Keeping the side edges of the pattern and leather aligned, turn them over so that the pattern is facing up.

26. Using a pencil, trace along the finger, thumb hole, and hem edges of the pattern. Then set aside the pattern.

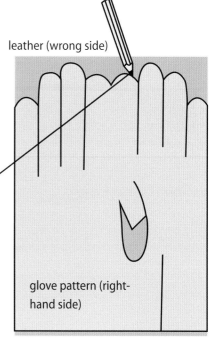

leather (wrong side)

glove pattern (right-hand side)

27. Using scissors, cut out the fingers and the thumb hole along the pencil lines. To cut the fingers, start by making straight slashes between the fingers; then trim around the tips.

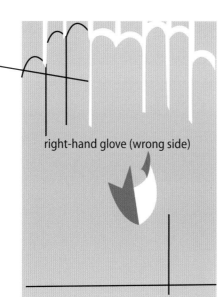

right-hand glove (wrong side)

31. Place the pattern on a flat surface so that the side marked "right-hand glove" is facing up, and repeat Steps 22–29 to cut the left glove.

28. Fold the glove in half lengthwise, wrong side out, and align the side edges.

29. Cutting both layers at once, trim along the hem cutting line. Then, if you are working on a wrist-length glove, cut the vent opening.

30. Mark the glove "right-hand glove."

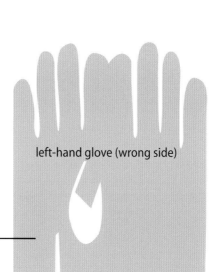

right-hand glove (wrong side)

left-hand glove (wrong side)

32. Set the glove pieces aside until they are thoroughly dry.

E: *Cutting out the thumb pieces*

33. Select a piece of the leather that is stretched in the direction opposite to the grain-line arrows. Cut a leather rectangle that is about 6½ inches long in the direction of the grain-line arrows and exactly 5½ inches wide in the other direction.

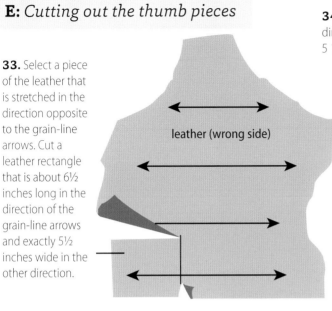

leather (wrong side)

34. Now stretch the leather piece in the direction of the grain-line arrows until the 5 1/2-inch width narrows to 3¼ inches.

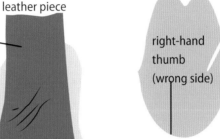

leather piece (wrong side)

35. Determine the width of the leather pieces you will need for cutting the thumbs. If you are making women's gloves, use 3¾ inches for size 6½; add ¼ inch for each half-size larger. If you are making men's gloves, use 4 inches for size 8 and under; add ¼ inch for each half-size larger.

36. Cut two pieces from the leather strip to the width you determined in Step 35.

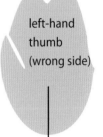

37. Stretch one leather piece in the direction opposite to the grain-line arrows until it is slightly narrower than the width of the thumb pattern.

38. Place the thumb pattern on a flat surface so that the side marked "left-hand thumb" is facing up. Lay one of the leather pieces, wrong side down, on the pattern so that the grain-line arrows are parallel.

39. Smooth and stretch the leather out until it is the same width as the pattern.

leather piece

thumb pattern (left-hand side)

right-hand thumb (wrong side)

left-hand thumb (wrong side)

40. Turn the pieces over so that the pattern is facing up. Then trace around the pattern, and cut out the thumb piece as you did the glove pieces. Mark the piece "right-hand thumb."

41. Repeat Steps 37–40 to cut out the left-hand thumb piece. Then set the pieces aside until they are thoroughly dry.

F: *Cutting the side finger pieces*

42. Using scraps of the leather that are already stretched in the direction opposite of the grain-line arrows, cut 12 strips of leather. Make sure the long edges of the strips are at right angles to the grain-line arrows. For men's gloves, the strips should be 6 inches long and ¾ inch wide. For women's gloves, they should be 5½ inches long and ½ inch wide.

43. Set the pieces aside until they are thoroughly dry.

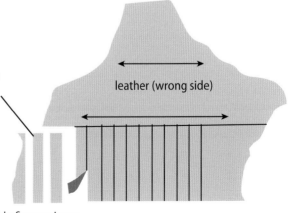

leather (wrong side)

side finger pieces

ASSEMBLING THE GLOVES

A: *Making the decorative stitching*

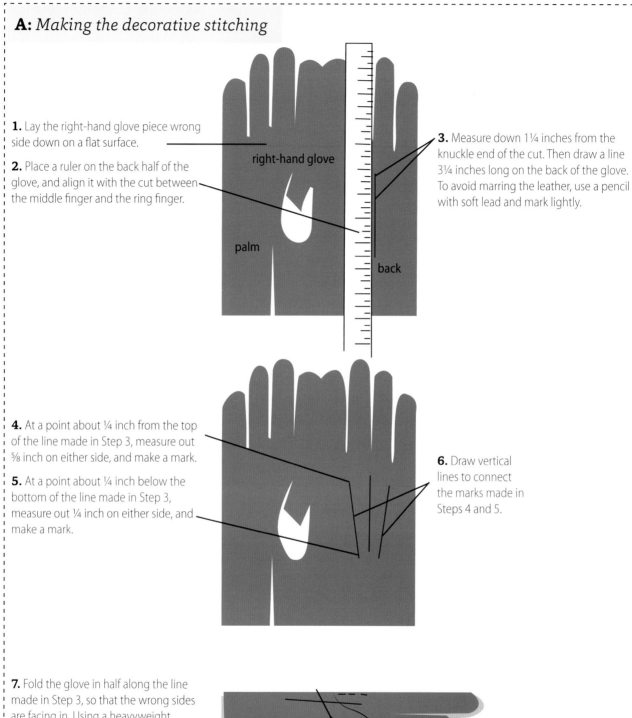

1. Lay the right-hand glove piece wrong side down on a flat surface.

2. Place a ruler on the back half of the glove, and align it with the cut between the middle finger and the ring finger.

3. Measure down 1¼ inches from the knuckle end of the cut. Then draw a line 3¼ inches long on the back of the glove. To avoid marring the leather, use a pencil with soft lead and mark lightly.

4. At a point about ¼ inch from the top of the line made in Step 3, measure out ⅝ inch on either side, and make a mark.

5. At a point about ¼ inch below the bottom of the line made in Step 3, measure out ¼ inch on either side, and make a mark.

6. Draw vertical lines to connect the marks made in Steps 4 and 5.

right-hand glove (wrong side)

7. Fold the glove in half along the line made in Step 3, so that the wrong sides are facing in. Using a heavyweight Size B cotton thread or three strands of embroidery floss twisted together, sew along the fold—⅛ inch away from the edge—as you would a tuck. Use a running stitch and insert the needle with a stabbing motion.

8. Stitch along the other two lines drawn in Step 6 in the same way.

B: *Inserting the thumb*

9. Fold the right-hand thumb piece in half lengthwise so that the wrong side is together and the side edges are aligned.

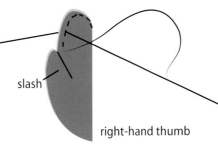

slash

right-hand thumb

10. Using the same thread as for the decorative stitching, sew the rounded tip and side edges together with a running stitch, ⅛ inch in from the edge. Start at the fold and sew down to the slash. Do not cut the thread, because you will resume sewing at this same point in the next step.

11. With the wrong sides together, align the lower edge of the slash on the thumb piece with the bottom edge of the flap in the thumb hole of the glove section. Make sure the edges are the same length and, if necessary, stretch one to fit. With the thread and needle that are still attached to the thumb piece, sew the thumb piece to the glove section along the lower edge of the glove flap. Use a running stitch ⅛ inch in from the edge.

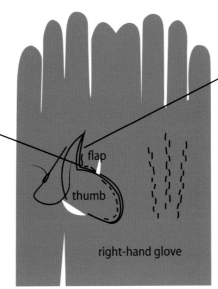

flap

thumb

right-hand glove

12. Next sew the other side of the thumb slash to the long side edge of the glove flap.

13. Finish by sewing the long curved edge of the thumb piece to the thumb hole of the glove, as shown, making sure to match them exactly. Adjust by stretching if necessary.

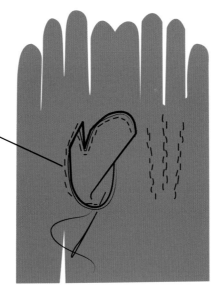

14. If you are making long flared gloves—which do not have hems—skip to Box D.

C: *Hemming the glove*

15. Lay the right-hand glove wrong side up on a flat surface.

16. To mark the hemline, measure down 1¼ inches from the bottom of the thumb hole, and draw a line at right angles to the side edges.

17. Apply a thin coat of rubber cement just above the hemline.

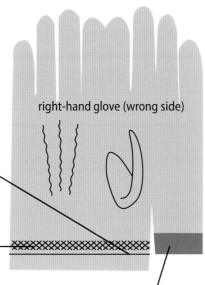

right-hand glove (wrong side)

18. Turn up the edge of the glove hem along the hemline.

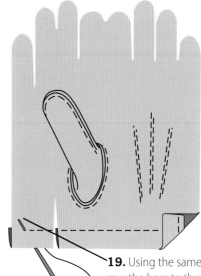

19. Using the same stitching thread, sew the hem to the glove with a running stitch, ⅛ inch below the raw edge of the hem.

D: *Attaching the side finger pieces*

20. With the wrong sides together, align the edge of one of the side finger pieces cut out in Box F (page 57) with the inner edge of the little finger on the back half of the glove. The side finger piece should extend ½ inch beyond the tip of the glove finger.

21. Using the heavyweight stitching thread, start at the center of the fingertip, and sew the side finger piece to the little finger with a running stitch, ⅛ inch in from the edge. Do not cut the thread.

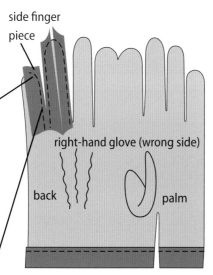

side finger piece

right-hand glove (wrong side)

back   palm

22. With the wrong sides together, align the edge of another side finger piece along the adjacent edge of the ring finger of the glove.

23. Make one stitch straight across the point of the cut, and sew the side finger piece to the ring finger. Stop at the center of the fingertip.

24. Sew another side finger piece to the other edge of the ring finger, taking one stitch back over your last stitch as you start.

25. Continuing in the same manner, sew the side finger pieces to both edges of the middle finger and the nearest edge of the index finger to the back half of the glove. At the tip of the index finger, stop and secure your thread.

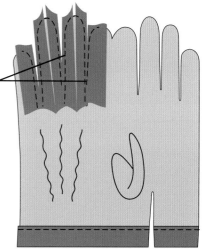

26. Fold each side finger piece in half, and trim the upper edge even with the curve of the fingertip, cutting through both layers at once.

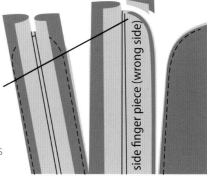

side finger piece (wrong side)

E: *Closing the fingers*

27. Partially turn the palm side of the glove over the back side, wrong sides together, to that the index finger is folded in half.

28. Using the heavyweight stitching thread, sew the tips of the index finger together until you reach the side finger piece. Sew ⅛ inch in from the edge, using a running stitch.

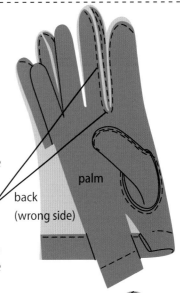

side piece

palm

back

right-hand glove (wrong side)

29. Catch the side piece with a stitch through its tip. Then close the index finger by sewing the unattached edges of the side piece and the finger together.

32. At the fingertip, make two whipstitches—one over the other—between the two side finger pieces to pull them tightly together. Similarly, make two whipstitches between the two glove finger pieces.

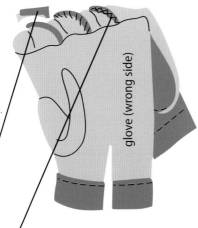

30. Continuing to fold the palm side of the glove over the back side, align the unattached edge of the next side finger piece with the adjacent edge of the middle finger on the palm of the glove. Be very careful to match the pieces at the fingertip.

31. Then take a stitch straight across the point of the cut, and sew the side finger piece and the finger together up to the center of the fingertip.

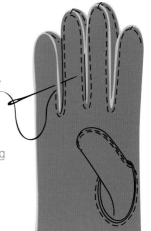

palm

back
(wrong side)

33. Continuing to fold the palm side of the glove over the back side, close the middle finger by sewing the unattached edges of the side finger pieces and the finger together.

34. Close the two remaining fingers in the same manner. Stop at the tip of the little finger, but do not cut the thread.

F: *Finishing the fingers*

35. Turn the glove—but not the fingers—wrong side out so that you can work on the unfinished lower edges of the fingers.

36. Trim the ends of the side finger pieces to within ⅛ inch of the stitches that attach them to the glove.

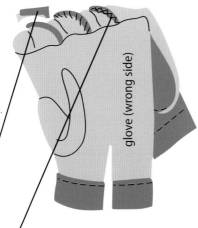

glove (wrong side)

37. Using regular mercerized cotton thread that matches the color of the leather, sew each pair of trimmed ends together with small whipstitches. Then sew back over them so that the stitches crisscross.

G: *Closing the glove*

38. Turn the glove right side out, and align the side edges.

39. Using the heavyweight stitching thread, sew the side edges together. Use a running stitch and sew ⅛ inch in from the edge. At the hem, finish with two whipstitches—one over the other.

40. If you are making long gloves—which do not have vents—skip to Box I.

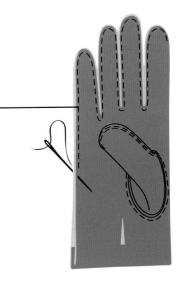

H: *Finishing the vent*

41. To make the binding for the vent, cut a strip of leather ¾ inch wide and 1 inch longer than twice the length of the vent opening.

42. Align the binding, wrong side up, along one edge of the opening.

43. Using regular mercerized cotton thread that matches the color of the leather, sew the edge of the binding to the edge of the opening with a small whipstitch. Start at the hem edge and sew to the point of the cut.

44. At the point make a ¼-inch clip in the outer edge of the binding.

45. Align the binding with the other edge of the cut, and continue sewing up to the hem edge

49. Trim the inner edge of the binding to within ⅛ inch of the running stitch.

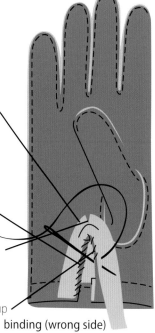

binding (wrong side)

46. Trim the excess binding even with the hem edge.

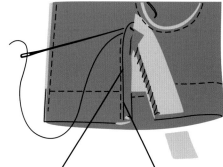

47. Turn under the binding so that it is inside the glove.

48. Using the heavyweight stitching thread, sew the binding to the glove with a running stitch, ⅛ inch inside the seam.

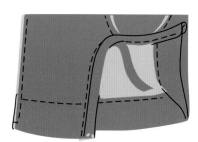

I: *Making the left-hand glove*

50. Make the decorative stitching, insert the thumb and turn up the hem on the left-hand glove as you did on the right-hand glove in Boxes A–C (pages 58–60).

51. To attach the side finger pieces, start by folding the glove index finger in half lengthwise and sewing the tips together from the fold to the center of the tip.

52. Then sew the side pieces to the fingers on the glove back as you did on the right-hand glove (Box O), but work in the opposite direction—from the index finger to the little finger.

53. Secure your thread at the center of the tip of the little finger.

54. Finish the left-hand glove as you did the right-hand glove (Boxes E–H). When you close the fingers this time, start at the center of the tip of the index finger.

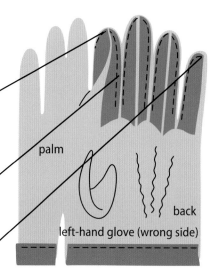

palm

back

left-hand glove (wrong side)

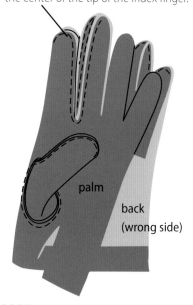

palm

back (wrong side)

Clutch with Snakeskin Trim

Made of beautiful materials, this clutch makes a stunning piece to compliment an outfit for an evening out. Lamb suede is recommended, although a lambskin or cabretta of similar delicacy can be substituted. The design makes a wonderful oversize clutch, although chain or another form of strap can be added to make a small shoulder bag.

Tools and Materials

- ❑ Suede
- ❑ Snakeskin
- ❑ Lining fabric
- ❑ Chain (optional)
- ❑ Metal rings or jump rings (optional)
- ❑ Tracing paper
- ❑ Pencil or marker
- ❑ Lightweight cardboard
- ❑ Masking tape
- ❑ Dressmaker's carbon paper
- ❑ Scissors
- ❑ Muslin
- ❑ Filler paper
- ❑ Pushpins
- ❑ Sewing pins

- ❑ Awl
- ❑ Utility knife
- ❑ Ruler
- ❑ Rubber cement
- ❑ Mallet
- ❑ Chalk
- ❑ Metal snap
- ❑ Snap setting tools
- ❑ Pellon interfacing
- ❑ Sewing machine
- ❑ Leather machine needle
- ❑ Thread to match
- ❑ Pliers

PREPARATION

Before you begin, you will need to use the patterns on pages 65–66 to create the pattern templates for your project. Using tracing paper, copy the outline of all of the pattern pieces on pages 65–66. Place the tracing paper, marked side up, on a piece of lightweight cardboard. Use tabs of tape to hold it in place.

Insert dressmaker's carbon paper between the tracing paper and the cardboard, and transfer the pattern outlines and all the pattern markings, including the notches, fold lines, and marks indicating the position for the snap, to the cardboard. Remove the tracing paper, and label each piece. Cut the patterns from the cardboard along the lines.

Enlarge all patterns 300%

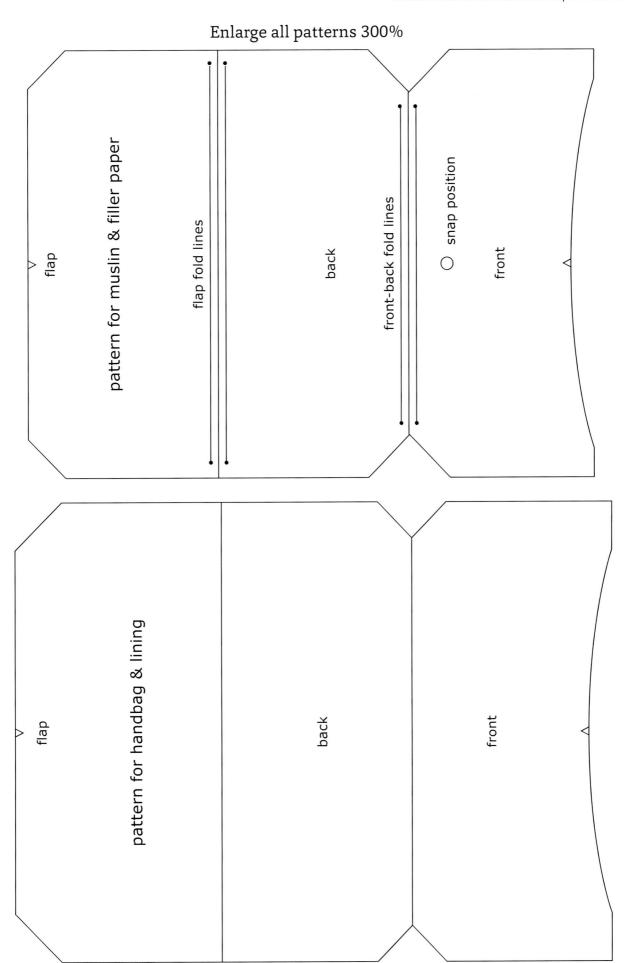

pattern for muslin & filler paper

flap

flap fold lines

back

front-back fold lines

snap position

front

pattern for handbag & lining

flap

back

front

Enlarge all patterns 300%

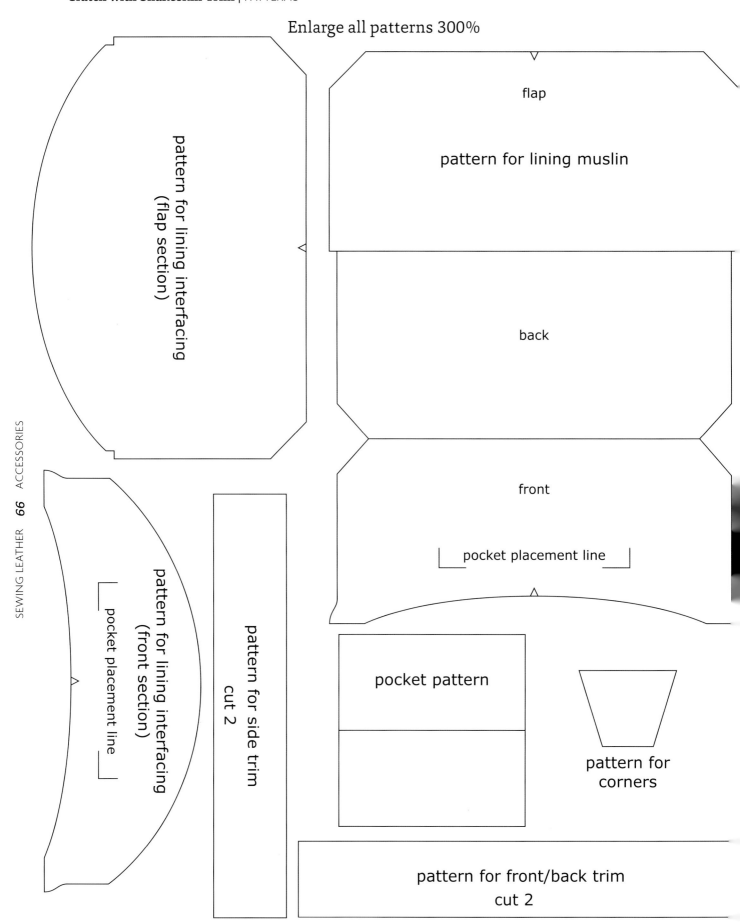

CUTTING OUT THE LEATHER AND THE STIFFENING

A: *Cutting out the leather pieces*

1. Lay the leather wrong side down on your work board.

2. Place the cardboard pattern on top of the leather and cut it out following the directions given on pages 17–19 for the type of leather you are using. Work first on the long edges, then cut the V-shaped wedges and diagonal corners.

3. Cut small notches in the leather to mark the position of the notches on the pattern.

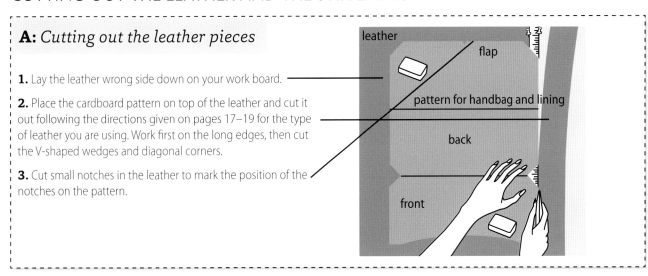

B: *Cutting out and marking the stiffening*

4. Cut 24-inch-by-18-inch rectangles of muslin and filler paper (a lightweight cardboard or heavyweight interfacing), making sure that the shorter side of the filler is parallel to the grain of the paper (the direction in which the paper rolls most easily is the direction of the grain).

5. Lay the muslin rectangle on your work board and place the filler paper on top of it.

9. Using an awl, punch a hole through the pattern and the filler paper beneath it at each end of the pattern markings for the fold lines between the front and back sections.

10. Mark the ends of the flap fold lines in the same manner.

11. Indicate the position for the front snap on the paper by punching a hole through the pattern marking for the snap.

12. Remove the pushpins and fold back a corner of the pattern and filler paper. Mark the underside of the paper and the upper side of the muslin with an X.

6. Place your pattern on top of the filler paper, and anchor it several inches in from the edges with pushpins.

7. Cut out the filler paper and the muslin at the same time.

8. Indicate the flap fold lines and the front-back fold lines with pencil on the filler paper. Then cut small notches in the filler paper and the muslin to mark the position of the notches on the pattern.

13. Set aside the pattern and the muslin and pin the filler paper, with the X-marked side down to your work board.

14. Draw a line connecting each pair of awl holes that were punched in Steps 9 and 10 to mark the ends of the flap fold lines and the front-back fold lines.

15. Using a utility knife and a ruler, slit the filler paper along each of the flap fold and front-back fold lines.

16. Draw an X through the hole punched in Step 11 to mark the position of the front snap.

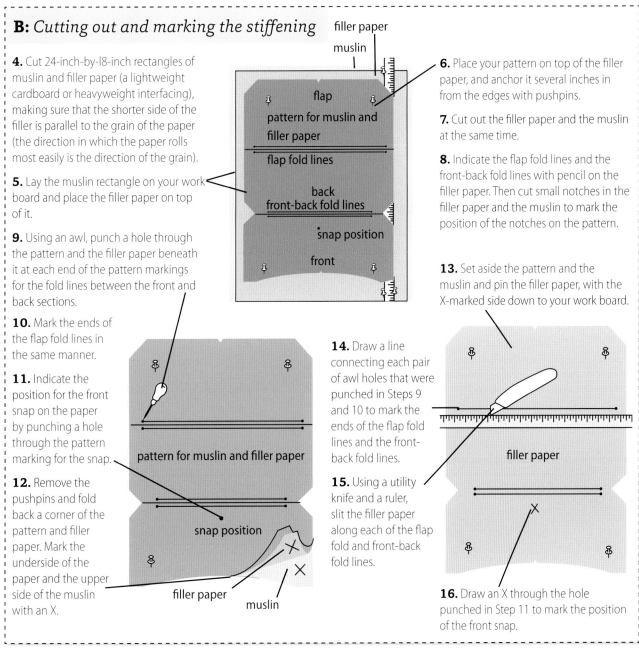

MAKING THE HANDBAG

A: *Attaching the stiffening to the leather*

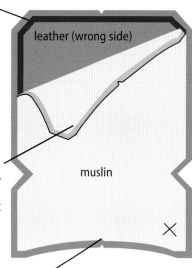

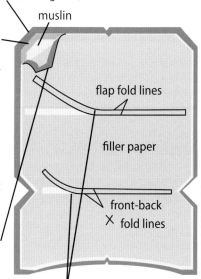

1. Place the leather wrong side up on your work board. Then brush a thin coat of rubber cement around all sides of the leather, 1 inch in from the edges. Let it dry.

2. Place the muslin, X-marked side down, on your work board and brush a thin coat of rubber cement around all the edges. Let it dry.

3. Place the glued side of the muslin on top of the leather, centering it so that the notches along the front and flap edges are aligned and the ½-inch edge of leather that protrudes is even all around.

4. Brush a thin coat of rubber cement along all edges of the muslin. Let it dry.

5. Place the filler paper, X-marked side up, on your work board and brush a thin coat of rubber cement along all the edges. Let it dry.

6. Place the glued side of the filler paper on top of the muslin, aligning all the edges.

7. To remove a narrow strip of the stiff filler paper along the flap fold line and the front-back fold line, take a utility knife and make a cut at both ends of the horizontal fold-line cuts made in Step 15. Be careful not to cut into the muslin and leather beneath the filler paper. Set aside the cut-out strips.

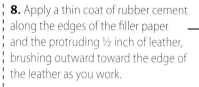
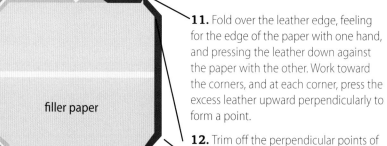

8. Apply a thin coat of rubber cement along the edges of the filler paper and the protruding ½ inch of leather, brushing outward toward the edge of the leather as you work.

9. After the rubber cement is dry, clip the protruding leather edge at each V-shaped wedge, cutting to within ⅛ inch of the point.

10. Trim the front corners diagonally ⅛ inch away from the paper. Then clip at ½-inch intervals around the curved front edge, cutting to within ⅛ inch of the paper.

11. Fold over the leather edge, feeling for the edge of the paper with one hand, and pressing the leather down against the paper with the other. Work toward the corners, and at each corner, press the excess leather upward perpendicularly to form a point.

12. Trim off the perpendicular points of leather at the corners with scissors.

13. To flatten and ensure a firm bond, hammer the leather down with a mallet.

B: *Preparing the snakeskin trim*

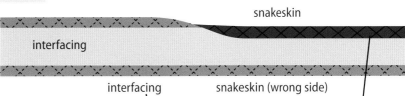

snakeskin

interfacing

interfacing   snakeskin (wrong side)

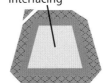

interfacing

snakeskin

14. Cut out the snakeskin and the interfacing, using the trim pattern pieces. Then trim away ½ inch along all sides of the interfacing for the wedge-shaped corners and along the long edges only of the interfacing strips.

15. Lay the snakeskin wrong side up. Brush rubber cement down the center of each strip and in the center of the wedges. Repeat on the interfacing.

16. Place the interfacing, glued sides down, on top of the matching snakeskin strips, centering them between the long edges and aligning the short ends. Center the wedge-shaped interfacing pieces on the matching snakeskin sections. Trim the snakeskin diagonally at the corners, cutting ⅛ inch from the interfacing.

17. Brush a light coat of rubber cement onto the protruding edges of the snakeskin and along all edges of interfacing. Let it dry.

18. Fold over one glued edge of the snakeskin strip for the front and sides and both glued edges of the strip for the back. Then, fold over all but the longest edge of each wedge. Press firmly against the interfacing, making sure that the corners are flat and even.

19. Brush a light coat of rubber cement over the entire wrong side of all sections of the trim.

C: *Attaching the trim to the handbag*

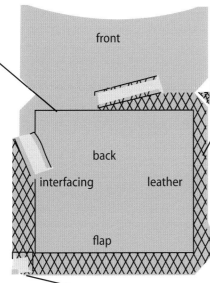

front

back

interfacing   leather

flap

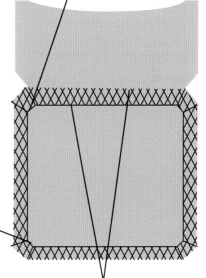

20. Place the finished leather handbag section wrong side down on your work board with the flap section nearest you.

21. Draw chalk lines 1¼ inches in from the edge—horizontally along the front edge of the flap and vertically along the side edges of the flap and back section—ending at the points of the V-shaped cutouts. Then draw a horizontal line across the leather 1¼ inches in from the cutouts, as shown.

22. Place the four snakeskin strips wrong sides down on the four corresponding edges of the flap and back section, aligning them with the chalk marks made in Step 21. This will leave a ½-inch overhang of snakeskin. Press the trim sections down to let the glue applied in Step 19 hold them temporarily in place.

23. Miter the corners of the border, folding back each snakeskin section diagonally and trimming off the folded-back portions.

24. Trim the corners of the trim so that they are flush with the diagonal corners of the handbag.

25. Turn under the ½-inch overhang of snakeskin to the wrong side of the handbag and press down.

26. Place the wedge-shaped corner sections of snakeskin on top of the glued-down trim on the right side of the handbag, aligning the inner corners. Press down firmly.

27. At the outer corners, turn under the ½-inch overhang of snakeskin to the wrong side of the bag.

28. Machine stitch the trim of the handbag along the sides of the wedges, as close to the edges as possible.

29. Machine stitch as close as possible to the outer edge of the trim along the back section only, beginning and ending at the points of the V-shaped cutouts. Then stitch all around the inner edge of the border, beginning and ending at the center back.

D: *Attaching the snap to the front section*

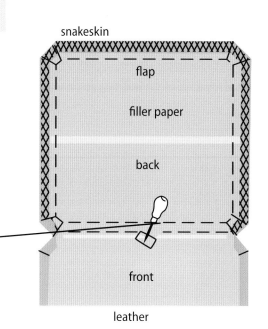

snakeskin

flap

filler paper

back

front

leather

30. Place the handbag wrong side up on your work board with the front section nearest you.

31. To reinforce the area where the snap will be applied, brush a thin coat of rubber cement onto the filler paper around the snap marking made in Step 16 on page 67.

32. Cut a ¾-inch-square reinforcement patch from filler paper and coat one side lightly with rubber cement. Let it dry.

33. Holding the glued side of the patch down, punch a hole in the center of the patch with an awl. Then push the awl through the filler paper, the muslin and the leather at the point of the snap marking. Slide the patch down the awl and press it in place against the filler paper. Remove the awl.

34. Apply a snap from the outside of the handbag, using the hole made in the previous step and following the directions on the package.

E: *Stitching the sides of the handbag*

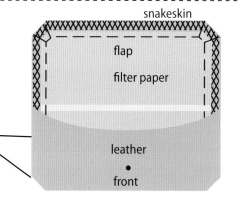

snakeskin

flap

filter paper

leather

front

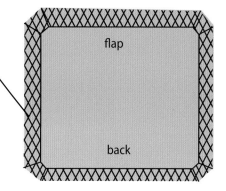

snakeskin

flap

back

35. Place the handbag wrong side up on your work board with the front section nearest to you.

36. Fold up the front section, aligning the edges and the diagonal bottom corners. Turn the bag over.

37. Machine stitch the sides of the handbag ⅛ inch in from the edge, sewing along the edge of the snakeskin trim through all layers. Start at the top of the front section by backstitching; then stitch down to the bottom of each diagonal corner.

LINING THE HANDBAG

A: *Cutting out the lining*

1. Cut 24-inch-by-18-inch rectangles of lining fabric and muslin and Pellon interfacing, which will serve as stiffening.

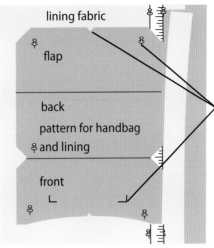

2. Attach the appropriate pattern pieces to the lining fabric, the lining muslin and the Pellon interfacing with pushpins and cut each out. Cut small notches to mark the position of the notches on the pattern. Mark the position of the inside pocket on the interfacing for the front section with chalk or pencil.

B: *Attaching the stiffening to the lining*

3. Place the lining muslin on your work board. Brush a thin coat of rubber cement onto the muslin around the flap edge and along the curved front edge.

4. Apply rubber cement to the outer edges of the interfacing for the flap and the front section. Let it dry.

5. Place the glued side of the interfacing on top of the lining muslin, matching the notches and aligning the edges.

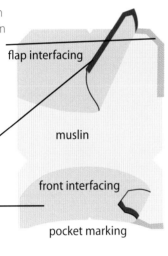

9. Place the interfaced muslin on top of the lining—interfaced side up—aligning the edges of the muslin with the chalk lines on the lining.

10. Clip the protruding lining at each end of the flap, cutting right up to the edge of the muslin.

11. Trim the excess lining on both sides of the back and front sections.

12. Trim the front corners diagonally ¼ inch from the muslin.

13. Clip into the lining on the curved front edge at ¼-inch intervals, cutting to ⅛ inch of the muslin.

6. Place the lining wrong side up on your work board and lay the muslin—interfaced side up—on top of it. Center the muslin so that the notches line up and an even amount of lining fabric protrudes all around. Then trace the outline of the muslin on the lining fabric with chalk. Set aside the muslin.

7. Brush a thin coat of rubber cement around the edges of the lining fabric just inside the chalk markings made in the previous step. Let it dry.

8. Brush a thin coat of rubber cement around the outer edges of the muslin side of the interfaced muslin. Let it dry.

14. Brush a thin coat of rubber cement onto the protruding lining fabric and the adjacent edges of the flap and front interfacing. Let the glue dry.

15. Fold over the lining edges and finish as you did for the handbag in Steps 11 and 12 on page 68.

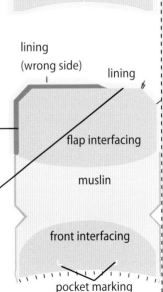

16. Mark the position for the inside pocket on the finished side of the lining by punching holes with an awl through all layers at each end of the markings. Then re-mark the position of the holes with chalk Xs on the outside of the lining.

C: *Preparing the inside pocket*

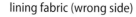
lining fabric (wrong side)

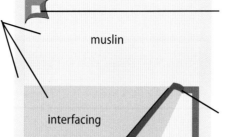
muslin

interfacing

17. Using the pocket pattern piece, cut a muslin pocket piece the exact size of the pattern. Cut another pocket piece out of the lining fabric, ½ inch larger than the pattern on all sides to provide for seam allowances. Then fold the pattern in half and cut out a third pocket section from the Pellon interfacing.

18. Lay the lining piece wrong side up on your work board. Center the muslin piece over the lining piece and glue the two sections together with rubber cement.

19. Glue the interfacing to the lower portion of the muslin.

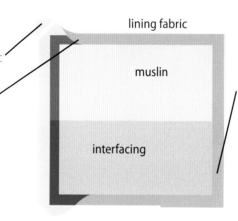
lining fabric

muslin

interfacing

20. Trim the corners of the lining fabric diagonally ¼ inch from the muslin.

21. Fold over the edges of the lining fabric protruding beyond the muslin and glue them to the muslin with rubber cement.

22. Brush a thin coat of rubber cement onto the folded-over edges of the lining and let it dry.

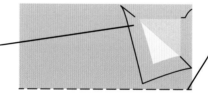

23. Fold the pocket section in half, wrong sides together, aligning the glued edges.

24. Machine stitch close to the folded edge as shown.

D: *Attaching the pocket to the lining*

25. Place the lining wrong side down on your work board. Lay the pocket on top of it, aligning the stitched edge of the pocket with the pocket placement markings. Pin in place.

26. Machine stitch the pocket to the lining around the three remaining edges. To reinforce the upper edges of the pocket, begin and end the stitching by making several backstitches beyond the upper edges onto the lining.

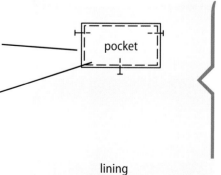
pocket

lining

E: *Joining the sides of the lining*

27. With the wrong sides out, fold the front section of the lining up against the back section, aligning the side edges. Pin in place.

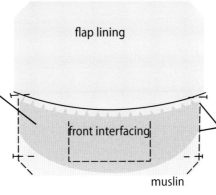

28. Machine stitch as follows: begin at one corner of the front edge and stitch across horizontally, as shown, for ¼ inch; then pivot and stitch down to the fold, sewing ⅛ inch in from the edge.

F: *Attaching the lining to the handbag*

29. Place the leather section of the handbag wrong side up on your work board with the flap section farthest from you. Brush a thin coat of rubber cement along the three edges of the flap; then apply rubber cement along the inside of the top edge of the front section, taking care not to mar the outside. Let the glue dry.

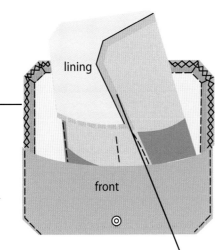

30. Apply rubber cement to the same three flap edges and top front edge of the lining. Let it dry.

31. Slip the lining into the handbag, first aligning and pressing together the front edges.

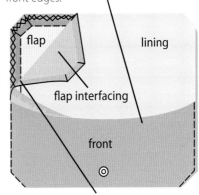

32. Then align and press together the flap edges of the handbag and the lining.

G: *Attaching the snap to the flap*

33. Fold down the lined flap over the front of the handbag and determine where on the lining flap the snap should be positioned in order to line up with the front snap. Punch a hole through the lining at this spot, using an awl.

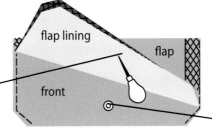

34. Pull the lining flap away from the handbag flap only as far as necessary to apply a reinforcement patch and a snap to the lining, following the directions on page 70, Box D, Steps 31–34. Then turn the lining flap up, realign the edges and press the layers together again.

H: *Finishing the handbag*

35. Hand stitch the handbag and lining together, using a running stitch or whipstitch, along the top edge of the front section. Begin and end ¾ inch away from the side seams and stitch ⅛ inch in from the edge. Turn the bag over.

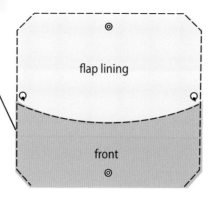

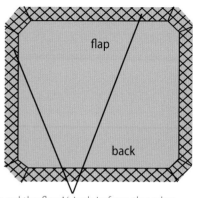

36. Machine stitch around the flap ¼ inch in from the edge. Begin and end by making several stitches over the ends of the side seams that were made on page 70, Box E, Step 37.

ATTACHING A CHAIN TO THE HANDBAG

A: *Sewing on the rings*

1. Using small fastening stitches, sew metal rings to the lining of the bag at both side edges, making sure that your stitches are made at the point where the flap will fold when the bag is closed.

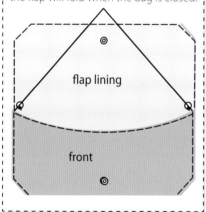

B: *Preparing the chain*

2. If the chain you are using has no opening, take a pair of pliers and gently open one link. You can also use a jump ring.

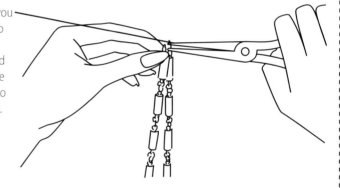

C: *Completing the chain*

3. Slip the chain through both rings once, as shown, or double it if a shorter handle is desired. Then refasten the link, using pliers again if necessary.

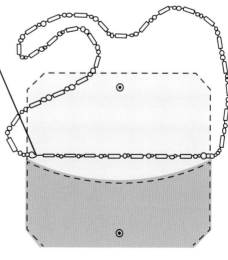

4. When completed, the chain can be used as a shoulder strap or slipped down inside the bag when the bag is carried as a clutch.

Basic Stitches

The diagrams below and on the following pages demonstrate how to make the elementary hand-sewing stitches referred to in this book.

SLIP STITCH

Fold under the hem edge and anchor the first stitch with a knot inside the fold. Point the needle to the left. Pick up one or two threads of the fabric close to the hem edge, directly below the first stitch, and slide the needle horizontally through the folded edge of the hem ⅛ inch to the left of the previous stitch. End with a fastening stitch.

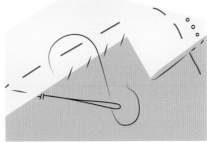

HEMMING STITCH

Anchor the first stitch with a knot inside the hem; then, pointing the needle up and to the left, pick up one or two threads of the garment fabric close to the hem. Push the needle up through the hem ⅛ inch above the edge; pull the thread through. Continue picking up one or two threads and making ⅛-inch stitches in the hem at intervals of ¼ inch. End with a fastening stitch.

OVERCAST STITCH

Draw the needle, with knotted thread, through from the wrong side of the fabric ⅛ to ¼ inch down from the top edge. With the thread to the right, insert the needle under the fabric from the wrong side ⅛ to ¼ inch to the left of the first stitch. Continue to make evenly spaced stitches over the fabric edge and end with a fastening stitch.

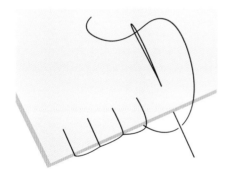

BLANKET STITCH

Using a knotted thread, bring the needle up from the bottom piece of fabric ¼ inch from the edge at the left side of the fabric. Pull it through. To make the first stitch, hold the thread down with your left thumb, and insert the needle just to the right of the point from which the thread emerged. Make sure the needle is at a right angle to the edge and goes over the thread before you draw the thread taut. For each succeeding stitch, repeat these steps but insert the needle into the fabric ¼ inch to the right of the preceding stitch. End with a fastening stitch.

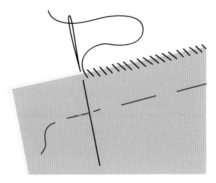

WHIPSTITCH

Using a knotted thread, draw the needle up from the bottom layer of fabric about ¹⁄₁₆ inch from the edge. Reinsert the needle—again from the bottom layer of fabric—about ¹⁄₁₆ inch to the left of the point from which the thread emerged, making sure the needle is at a right angle to the edge. Continue to make tiny, slanted, even stitches over the fabric edge. End with a fastening stitch.

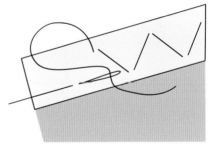

ZIGZAG STITCH

To attach tape to a piece of fabric, use knotted thread and make tiny, even, horizontal stitches going through the tape and picking up only a few threads of the fabric. Make the first stitch ⅛ inch from one edge of the tape and the next stitch ⅛ inch from the other edge, so that the thread stretches diagonally across the tape between the stitches. Continue alternating from one edge to the other, keeping the stitches at least ¼ inch apart, depending on the width of the tape. End with a fastening stitch.

Glossary

Backstitch: To reinforce the beginning or end of a seam by making several machine stitches back over the seam line.

Baste: To stitch together pieces of fabric temporarily, or to indicate pattern markings on both sides of a piece of fabric.

Bias: A line running diagonally to the threads in a woven fabric. A 45° bias is called a true bias.

Bias tape: A folded strip of nylon, rayon or cotton, cut diagonally to the fabric threads, i.e., on the bias, so that the strip will stretch smoothly to cover curved and straight edges of a garment piece. Double-fold bias tape is called bias binding; commonly made of cotton or a cotton-synthetic blend, it is used to bind raw edges.

Dart: A stitched fold, tapering to a point at one or both ends, used to shape fabric around curves.

Eyelet: A small round hole made in fabric for a cord tie or for ventilation. Also, the metal ring that reinforces such a hole.

Facing: A piece of fabric that is sewn along the raw edge of an opening such as a neckline and then turned to the inside to give the edge a smooth finish. Facings are usually cut from the same cloth as the garment itself.

Fastening stitch: A stitch used to anchor a thread by making three or four stitches, one over the other, in the same place.

Felt: A nonwoven fabric made from fibers that are matted together. Because its bulk and stiffness are similar to that of leather and suede, it is especially suitable for making prototypes for styling and fitting garments that are to be made of those materials.

Flat-felled seam: A double-stitched seam used on synthetic leathers to create the look of a lapped seam. One seam allowance is trimmed so that the opposite seam allowance can be turned and stitched on top of it to give a finished effect on both sides of the garment.

Fusible web tape: An adhesive tape used to attach interfacings and to reinforce areas of wear. The heat of an iron fuses the tape to fabrics without the need for sewing.

Glover's needle: A three-sided, wedge-like needle used for stitching leather.

Grain: In woven fabrics, the grain is the direction of the threads: the warp (the threads running from one cut end to the other) forms the lengthwise grain; the woof, or weft (the threads running across the lengthwise grain from one finished edge to the other) forms the crosswise grain. In leather, the grain is the direction of the most give or stretch. In paper, the grain is the direction in which the paper rolls more easily.

Grain-line arrow: The double-ended arrow printed on a pattern piece indicating how the piece should be aligned with the grains of the fabric.

Interfacing: A fabric sewn between two layers of fabric in a project to stiffen and strengthen the support parts of the project.

Lapped seam: For leather, a seam made by aligning the trimmed seam line of one piece of leather over the seam allowance and along the seam line of another piece, and then topstitching ⅛ inch in from the trimmed edge. A second row of topstitches is then made ¼ inch from the first line of stitching.

Lining: A fabric covering the inside of part or all of a garment.

Nap: The short fibers on the surface of a fabric that are pulled and brushed in one direction. Also, the rough surface on suede.

Nap layout: A cutting direction on patterns to indicate how the pattern is to be aligned with fabrics that, because of their surface, nap or printed design, change in appearance with the direction in which they are set. When such fabrics are used, all pattern pieces must be laid out and cut in one direction—with the nap.

Notch: A V- or diamond-shaped marking made on the edge of a garment piece as an alignment guide; intended to be matched with a similar notch or group of notches on another piece. Also a triangular cut made in the seam allowance of a curved seam to help it lie flat.

Pivot: A technique for machine stitching around angular corners that involves stopping the machine, with the needle down, at the apex of a corner, raising the presser foot, pivoting the fabric and then lowering the presser fool before continuing to stitch.

Plain seam: The joining of two pieces of fabric by placing the right sides together and stitching along the seam-line marking; the seam allowances are then usually pressed open.

Presser foot: The part of a sewing machine that holds down fabric while it is being advanced under the needle. An all-purpose, or general-purpose, foot has two prongs of equal length and is used for most stitching. A roller presser foot has two rollers with grids to prevent bulky or sheer fabric from sticking or slipping while stitching. A straight-stitch foot has one long and one short prong and can be used for straight stitching and stitching fabrics of varying thicknesses. A zipper foot has only one prong and is used to stitch zippers and cording.

Pressing cloth: A piece of fabric, preferably cotton drill cloth, that is placed between the iron and the garment when pressing.

Seam tape: A flat tape of finishing fabric—rayon or nylon with a woven edge, or nylon or polyester stretch lace—usually ½ to ⅝ inch wide, that is sewn over a seam to reinforce it or is used to finish hems.

Skiving: The technique of shaving leather, with a safety bevel or skiving tool, to make it less bulky, usually along edges to be seamed.

Tailor's chalk: Flat squares of wax, stone or clay, used to transfer pattern markings or adjustments onto fabric.

Tailor's ham: A firm, ham-shaped cushion used for pressing areas that require special shaping.

Tension: The degree of tightness of the two threads forming machine stitches.

Throat plate: A flat metal piece with a hole through which a sewing-machine needle passes as it stitches. Most throat plates have guidelines marked on both the left and the right sides to help keep seams straight.

Topstitching: A line of machine stitching on the visible side of a project, parallel to a seam.

Zigzag stitch: A serrated line of machine stitching.

Index

Note: Page numbers in *italics* indicate projects.

More Great Books from Design Originals

**Handmade Leather
Bags & Accessories**
ISBN 978-1-57421-716-2 **$19.99**
DO5036

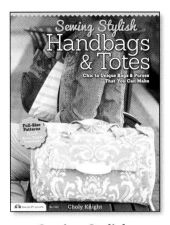

**Sewing Stylish
Handbags & Totes**
ISBN 978-1-57421-422-2 **$22.99**
DO5393

Sew Me! Sewing Basics
ISBN 978-1-57421-423-9 **$19.99**
DO5394

Sew Me! Sewing Home Décor
ISBN 978-1-57421-504-5 **$14.99**
DO5425

Pyrography Basics
ISBN 978-1-57421-505-2 **$9.99**
DO5426

Sewing Pretty Little Things
ISBN 978-1-57421-611-0 **$19.99**
DO5301

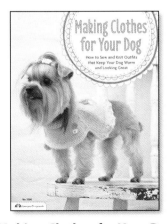

Making Clothes for Your Dog
ISBN 978-1-57421-610-3 **$19.99**
DO5300

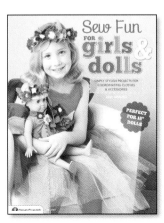

Sew Fun for Girls & Dolls
ISBN 978-1-57421-364-5 **$11.99**
DO3487

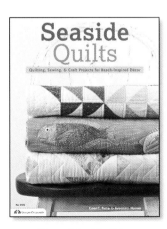

Seaside Quilts
ISBN 978-1-57421-431-4 **$24.99**
DO5402